First
Cake
Decorating

First
Cake
Decorating

Simple cake designs for beginners

COLLINS & BROWN

Contents

How to use this book **6**

Getting Started
8

Ingredients
14

BASIC TECHNIQUES
16

Victoria Sponge
22

Chocolate Victoria
Sponge **23**

Rich Fruit Cake
24

Carrot Cake
27

Madeira Cake
28

Marble Cake
30

Cupcakes
31

Icing and Frosting
Recipes **32**

COVERING CAKES
36

Banana Cake
50

Simnel Cake
52

Graduation Cake
54

Fresh Flower
Wedding Cake **56**

Classic Christmas
Cake **58**

PIPING
60

Ballet Cake
70

Secret Garden
Cupcakes **72**

Firework Cupcakes
74

Dinosaur Cake
76

Raspberry Ripple
Cupcake **78**

MODELLING
80

Rosebud Wedding
Cake **96**

Baby Bunny
Christening Cake **98**

Toadstool
100

Handbag Cake
102

Jungle Cake
104

USING CHOCOLATE
AND SUGAR **106**

Chocolate Birthday
Cake
116

Easter Chocolate
Fudge Cake
118

Coffee and Praline
Celebration Gateau
120

Black Forest
Roulade
122

White Chocolate and
Orange Wedding
Cake **124**

Suppliers **126**

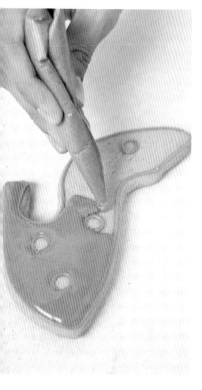

How to use this book

Cake decorating has changed remarkably over recent years – for instance, sugar crafting was once a work of art only be tackled by experts, but there are now many more tools available now, and with a little know-how, anything is possible. Just remember that when you are making any kind of celebration cake it is important to plan ahead and decide on the type of cake, its size and what type of decoration you want before you even begin to start baking.

Things to consider
- Your skill level and the time available – if you are inexperienced don't be too ambitious. It's better to create a simple design perfectly than a complicated one badly, or to make a design in too much of a rush so you have to cut corners.
- Who the cake is for – they might have a preference for a type of cake, or an interest or hobby that you can use as a starting point for your design.
- The occasion – is it formal or informal? How big will the cake need to be to serve everyone? If there is a theme you may need to fit in with it.
- When and where – can the cake be made some time in advance or does it have to be made immediately beforehand? Will the cake be transported and require last minute assembly?

This book is divided into sections: first we have Getting Started, which explains what you need in the way of basic baking equipment and ingredients, followed by Basic Techniques, which covers essential preparation as well as the recipes for a collection of classic cakes. The decorating part of the book has three sections: Covering Cakes, which details how to cover cakes in various ways along with some simple decoration techniques; Piping, which looks at all types of piped decoration; Modelling, using either sugarpaste (gumpaste), flowerpaste, almond paste (marzipan) or crystallized flowers; and finally Using Chocolate and Sugar, which shows you how to dip, mould shapes and create spun sugar items. Each section finishes with a collection of projects that put into practice the techniques detailed in the chapter. Each of the techniques is numbered and the same reference number is given in the project whenever the technique appears so you can refer back if you need to.

Filled with detailed description, helpful step-by-step instructions, endless pictures and many triple-tested recipes, this book is all you need to discover the joys of creating your own wonderful cakes for all occasions.

Getting started

Not much in the way of specialist equipment is needed for baking, although one or two items in particular – such as a food processor and electric whisk (mixer) – will make life much easier. Remember that kitchen equipment is subject to a great deal of wear and tear, so look for good-quality items.

Basic equipment

1 Scales (kitchen scale)
Accurate measurement is essential when following most baking recipes. The electronic scale is the most accurate and usually weighs in increments of 1–5g. Buy one with a flat platform on which you can put your bowl or measuring jug. Always set the scale to zero before adding the ingredients and use either metric or imperial measurements; do not mix them.

2 Measuring jugs, 3 cups and 4 spoons
Jugs can be plastic, metal or glass and are available in various sizes marked with both metric and imperial measures. Measuring cups are classically used in American recipes and are usually bought as sets of ¼, ⅓, ½ and 1 cups. It is essential to use calibrated measuring spoons in all baking recipes. Do not be tempted to reach into the cutlery drawer since general spoons used in the kitchen may vary in size, which will affect the accuracy of the recipe. If you don't have any measuring spoons, then go by the rule that 1 tbsp is equal to 15ml, and 1 tsp is equal to 5ml. Measuring spoons can be plastic, ceramic or metal and often come in sets attached together.

5 Mixing bowls
A selection of small, medium and large bowls are essential for good cake making. Choose bowls in glass, plastic, china or stainless steel with smooth, rounded insides for thorough and even mixing. Stainless steel bowls work best when you need to chill a mixture down quickly in the fridge or heat it up over simmering water (when melting chocolate, for example). Do not use stainless steel bowls in the microwave. Plastic or glass bowls are best if you need to use them in the microwave.

6 Mixing spoons
For general mixing, the cheap and sturdy wooden spoon is best. The spoon should be stiff, so that it can cope with thick mixtures. A large metal spoon for folding items together is also invaluable.

7 Spatulas
Essential for scraping out all the mixture from mixing bowls. The best have a silicone head, which moulds easily to the bowl. Also useful for folding ingredients together.

8 Sieves
A variety of fine wire mesh or nylon sieves are always needed to strain out ingredients or aerate dry ingredients, such as flour, cocoa powder and icing sugar.

9 Wire whisk
A flexible wire whisk is necessary for whisking all types of mixtures to obtain volume and give smooth consistencies. Generally, the larger the whisk the more efficient it is.

10 Palette knife (metal spatula)
For basic baking, a simple large straight-bladed palette knife will do most jobs. Ideal for loosening

cakes from tins (pans) and spreading and smoothing icing.

⓫ Brushes

For general glazing, brushes are available in many sizes with bristle or silicone tips. Take care as bristle brushes can moult when they get old, or become stiff if not cleaned properly.

⓬ Rolling pin

Essential for even rolling of pastry, dough, sugarpaste (gumpaste), and so on. Rolling pins come in different lengths, thicknesses and materials. Wooden varieties are generally cheap and universally effective, whereas silicone pins are more costly but ideal if rolling lots of pastry or sugarpaste, as they give a more even appearance.

⓭ Ruler or ⓮ tape measure and ⓯ scissors (kitchen shears)

Accurate measurement during cake baking and decorating is essential to guarantee good results. Sharp kitchen scissors are frequently needed for cutting out cake tin (pan) lining papers, templates, florists wire, etc.

⓰ Vegetable peeler

Choose one that fits your hand comfortably, either swivel-headed or y-shaped.

⓱ Graters

Either box or hand-held, graters are mostly used in baking for grating citrus zest or chocolate. Look for sturdy models that are comfortable to hold, as they will need to withstand pressure. Graters give coarse, medium-coarse or fine results.

⓲ Cake tins (pans)

The right cake tins are invaluable when it comes to baking all types of cakes. They vary in the quality and thickness of the metal, the finish, the sizing and the depth, so care must be taken when choosing them – try to buy the best quality you can afford. Tins may be single-piece, loose-bottomed or springform. Always measure the tin with a ruler across the base to ascertain its size. Never be temped to use a different shape or size of tin than the recipe states, otherwise the baking time, texture, depth and appearance of the cake will be affected.

⓳ Baking trays/baking sheets

These have many uses in baking and either have a lipped edge or are completely flat. Choose ones that are large (but which fit comfortably in your oven) to avoid having to bake in batches. Buy the best you can afford to avoid any warping when in contact with heat.

⓴ Wire racks

Available in different sizes and shapes, with wide or narrow mesh.

㉑ Knives

Small, medium and large knives with straight and serrated blades are needed for preparing ingredients and cutting cakes into layers.

㉒ Papers

There are a variety of papers, such as greaseproof (wax), non-stick baking parchment, waxed paper, rice paper and brown paper, which all have their uses. Greaseproof paper is suitable for lining cake tins (pans). Non-stick baking parchment is ideal for meringues, spreading melted chocolate, drying moulded or cut-out sugar decorations – in short, ensuring nothing sticks. Waxed paper is fine and flexible and is ideal for icing run-outs and to trace over designs for piped decorations. Rice paper is used for biscuits and macaroons; it adheres to the mixture, can be baked and is edible. Brown paper is used to fit around the outside of cake tins to protect the cake during long periods of baking.

㉓ Other useful bakeware

Loaf tins (pans), tart tins (fluted and plain), sandwich tins, pie tins, muffin tins. Reusable, non-stick, silicone baking mats and liners, muffin trays and cupcake moulds.

Decorating equipment

㉔ Palette knives (not shown)
Small straight and crank-handled palette knives/metal spatulas are ideal for lifting and transferring small and fragile icing decorations, spreading royal icing on to cakes and smoothing to the edges.

㉕ Piping (decorating) bags
Indispensable for piping icings and meringues. The most convenient are the disposable type – try to buy ones with added grip. Alternatively, use the nylon type, but make sure that you wash it very thoroughly in hot soapy water after each use.

㉖ Piping (decorating) pumps
Icing pumps are usually sold as part of an icing set, complete with nozzles (tips). They are made of metal or polythene and consist of a large tube with an interchangeable screw nozzle at one end and a plunger at the other end. The plunger unscrews for easy refilling and the pump dismantles for hygienic cleaning. The disadvantage of the icing pump is that you cannot 'feel' how the icing is reacting to the pressure applied to the plunger – this may result in too little or too much icing being pushed through the nozzle at the other end. Also, it is essential that the consistency of the icing is correct for good results.

㉗ Piping nozzles (tips)
Basic piping work can be achieved with just a few nozzles (check the recipe for the size of nozzle needed – often numerical). More sophisticated piping will require a large selection of piping nozzles, with varying tip sizes and shapes.

㉘ Cake boards
Available in many shapes, sizes and colours, cake boards give a professional finish to your cake. The larger the cake, the thicker and more substantial the board needs to be.

㉙ Cake smoothers
These help to smooth the surface of sugarpaste to obtain a satin-smooth finish and to eliminate cracks or imperfections.

㉚ Sugarpaste (gumpaste) modelling tools
Cutting knife, cone, bone and ball tools all have a purpose when working with sugarpaste, and for experimental cake decorators are well worth buying.

㉛ Sugarpaste (gumpaste) mats
These non-stick mats often come with pre-marked circles and grids for accurate, mark-free rolling. Textured mats are also available.

㉜ Fine brushes
Fine artist's brushes are available in many different shapes and sizes and are useful for painting with food colourings. Also useful when making run-outs.

㉝ Foam pads (shaping foam)
Cheap to buy and essential for supporting sugar, gum- and flowerpaste decorations and enabling them to dry in the correct shape.

㉞ Run-out film
This fine transparent plastic film can be used for making accurate run-out decorations, which slide easily off the film when they are dry. It may not be easy to source, however.

㉟ Scribing needle
Used for etching lines onto the surface of iced cakes in order to transfer designs from templates.

㊱ Crimpers
These tweezer-style tools have decorative end pieces that imprint various designs on the surface of sugarpaste.

㊲ Small acrylic rolling pin
Great for smoothly rolling out small quantities of icing and creating frills, petals and waves.

38 Craft knife

Ideal for cutting out shapes made from sugarpaste (gumpaste) and for veining leaves.

39 Embossing stamps (imprinters and impression mats)

Stamps that have raised designs of flowers, motifs, letters, or seasonal emblems are ideal. They are used to transfer designs onto sugarpaste.

40 Florist's (covered) wire

Available in gauges from very fine to thick, usually coated in white, green or brown tape. Used in sugarcraft for wiring flowers or leaves into sprays.

41 Stamens

Usually sold in bundles, stamens make up the centre of non-edible sugarcraft flowers. A vast variety is available, in different colours, sizes and finishes, to suit all sugarcraft flowers.

42 Ribbon slotters and insertion blades

These are great for making neat slits in the surface of sugarpaste (gumpaste), and then helping to insert the ribbons into the slits.

43 Thermometer

An accurate sugar thermometer is needed for testing the temperature of sugar syrup when making some icings, as well as for tempering chocolate.

44 Turntable

Turntables are comprised of a heavy base and a flat top that rotates. There are many qualities to choose from. They are essential for evenly turning a cake while icing and decorating to get good results.

45 Straight edge

This is a long, inflexible metal ruler that is used to obtain a smooth, flat finish on the surface of a royal iced cake. There are different lengths available, but a 30.5cm (12in) straight edge is easy to handle on cakes up to 25.5cm (10in).

46 Side scrapers

These are used to smooth royal icing on the side of cakes. They are made from plastic or stainless steel. They are also available patterned with ingrained patterns, to give a variety of designs to the sides of the cake.

47 Pillars and **48** dowels

Cake pillars (either hollow or solid) separate the layers of a tiered cake, but they don't always have to be used. Dowels, which are usually acrylic, are inserted into sugarpasted (gumpasted) cakes to support the tiers, as the icing alone is not strong enough. They are hygienic and trimmed to the level of the cake.

Cutters (not shown)

A set of plain round and fluted metal cutters have many uses in cake decorating. Fancy flower, leaf, novelty or biscuit cutters are available in many shapes and sizes, and you'll find endless uses for them. Plunge cutters, which eject the sugarpaste (gumpaste) shape by use of a spring plunger, are wonderfully easy to use and give professional results.

Icing (flower) nails (not shown)

These look like small upturned saucers of metal or polythene mounted on a nail – like mini turntables. They are held in the hand, and used as a rotating surface when piping flowers. A little icing is spread on the surface of the nail and a small square of non-stick or waxed paper is placed on top. The flower is then piped on to the paper, the nail being easily rotated as each petal is piped.

Ingredients

There are limited ingredients in cake making, so it is important to use the highest quality you can, and ensure that they are at the right temperature.

Fat

Unsalted butter generally gives the best results in most cake recipes. Margarine can be substituted in many recipes, although it doesn't lend such a good flavour. Low-fat spreads, with their high water content, are not suitable. For most cake recipes, you need to use the fat at room temperature. If necessary, soften it (cautiously) in the microwave.

Eggs

Eggs should be stored in the fridge in their box, but used at room temperature; if taken straight from the fridge they are more likely to curdle a cake mixture.

Note – Make sure you use the correct size eggs – unless otherwise stated, in the UK you should use medium eggs in all the recipes, while the equivalent size in the US would be large eggs. Where large eggs are specified, extra-large eggs should be used in the US.

To test whether eggs are fresh

Eggs frequently outlast their stated best before date, so do this test to see if they are still usable. Fill a bowl with cold water. One by one put your eggs into the water. Fresh eggs will sink to the bottom and lie either on their side or on their tip. If the egg floats it has gone off, so discard it.

Sugar

Lots of sugars can be used in cake making. Caster sugar (either white or golden), icing (confectioners') sugar, light and dark soft brown sugars and light or dark brown muscovado (brown) sugars are all common. Unrefined sugars give the best flavour.

Flour

Both plain (all-purpose) and self-raising (self-rising) white flours are commonly used in cake making. Wholemeal (wholewheat) flours give a denser texture and nuttier flavour. As white and wholemeal flours behave slightly differently when it comes to liquid absorption, never simply substitute wholemeal flour in a recipe stating plain flour. You can convert plain flour into self-raising flour by adding 1 tsp baking powder to every 125g/4oz/⅞ cup of flour.

Baking powder

This is a raising agent consisting of an acid, usually cream of tartar, and an alkali, such as bicarbonate of soda (baking soda). It is activated when it gets wet and produces carbon dioxide. This expands during baking and makes cakes and breads rise. Some baking powders are also heat activated.

Dried fruit

Dried fruits are classified into vine fruits and tree fruits. Their moisture content is reduced by drying and the character of the fruits changes completely, becoming wrinkled, leathery and sweet. Always check on the packet whether the dried fruit needs any preparation or whether it is ready to eat.

Nuts

Some nuts can be bought ready prepared, others need preparation. After nuts have been shelled, they are still coated with a thin, papery skin, which although edible, tastes a little bitter. This is easier to remove if the nuts are blanched or toasted.

To blanch – Put the shelled nuts into a bowl and cover with boiling water. Leave for 2 minutes, then drain. Remove the skins by rubbing the nuts in a tea towel or squeezing them between your thumb and index finger.

To toast – Toasting nuts improves their flavour. Preheat the oven to 200°C (180°C fan oven)/400°F/ Gas mark 6. Put the shelled nuts on a baking sheet in a single layer and toast for 8–15 minutes in the oven until the skins are beginning to toast. When cool enough to handle, remove the skins by rubbing the nuts in a tea towel or by squeezing them firmly between your thumb and index finger.

To chop – Nuts are usually used chopped for cake mixtures and the quickest way to achieve this is to pulse them in a food processor. Alternatively, chop them on a board with a cook's knife.

Essences and extracts

Essences and extracts with flavours such as vanilla and almond make frequent appearances in cake making. Extracts are, in general, higher quality than essences and deliver a more natural flavour. If using essences, look for ones labelled 'natural', rather than 'flavouring'.

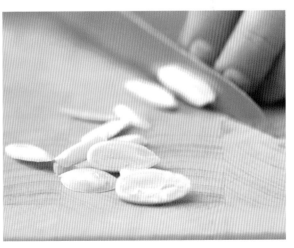

Basic Techniques

Use this section to prepare and create a series of classic cakes to cover – all the recipes are triple-tested, but you can also use your own favourite cake recipes. This section also includes recipes for different icings and frostings.

1 Lining tins

Unless otherwise stated, line tins (pans) with greaseproof (wax) paper (use baking parchment for roulades) to help stop the cake sticking to the sides of the tin or burning. Lightly grease the inside of the tin first to keep the paper in place. Apply the butter or oil with kitchen paper (paper towels) – do not thickly grease the edges of the cake; you need just enough to hold the paper in place. Once the tin is lined, grease the paper lightly.

Lining a square tin

This method works well for larger square tins. For small tins use one long strip instead of four separate side panels.

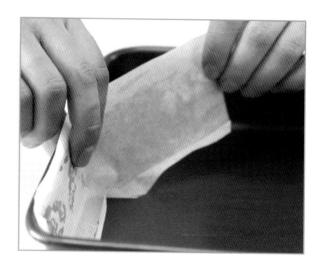

1   Put the tin (pan) base-down on greaseproof (wax) paper and draw around it. Cut out the square just inside the drawn line. Measure the length and depth of one side of the tin. Cut four strips of greaseproof paper to this length, each about 2cm/¾in wider than the depth of the tin. Fold up one long edge of each strip by 1cm/½in. Lightly grease the inside of the tin with butter. Position the four strips in the tin, with the folded edge lying on the bottom.

2   Lay the square on the bottom of the tin, then lightly grease the paper, taking care not to move the side strips.

Lining a round tin

1 Put the tin (pan) base-down on greaseproof (wax) paper and draw around it. Cut out the circle just inside the drawn line. Cut a long strip about 2cm/¾in wider than the depth of the tin, and long enough to wrap around the outside of the tin. Fold up one long edge of the strip by 1cm/½in. Make cuts about 2.5cm/1in apart, through the folded edge of the strip(s) up to the fold line.

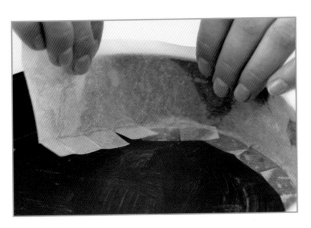

2 Lightly grease the inside of the tin with butter. Press the strip to the inside of the tin, making sure the snipped edges sit on the bottom. Trim any overlap once inside the tin. Lay the circle in the bottom of the tin, then lightly grease the paper.

Lining a Swiss roll tin

Put the tin (pan) in the centre of a large sheet of greaseproof (wax) paper or baking parchment and trim the paper 2.5cm/1in wider than the tin on all sides. Still with the tin in place, cut from one corner of the paper to the closest corner of the tin. Repeat with the remaining corners. Lightly grease the inside of the tin with butter. Fit the paper into the tin, neatly pressing into the corners. Lightly grease the paper. Alternatively, you can cut into the corners of the paper once it has been pressed into the tin.

Lining shaped tins

Put the tin (pan) base-down on greaseproof (wax) paper, draw around it and cut out. Measure and cut a strip of greaseproof paper to fit around the outside of the tin. Lightly grease the inside of the tin with butter, then line the base and sides with the pieces of paper and grease again.

2 Mixing methods

A wide variety of cakes can be prepared using just three basic mixing techniques: creaming, all-in-one and whisking.

Creaming

Put the butter and sugar into a large bowl and beat together until pale and fluffy. Add the eggs, one at a time, beating well after each addition and adding a spoonful of flour to the mixture if it looks as if it's about to curdle. Using a large metal spoon, fold in the remaining flour.

All-in-one

Place all the ingredients into a bowl and mix together until smooth.

Whisking

Put the eggs and sugar into a large heatproof bowl and, using a hand-held electric mixer, whisk until well blended. Put the bowl over a pan of hot water and whisk until pale and creamy and thick enough to leave a trail on the surface when the whisk is lifted. Remove the bowl from the pan and continue to whisk until cool and thick.

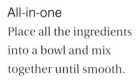

3 Testing if cakes are cooked

Ovens vary and the time given in the recipe might be too short or too long to correctly cook what you are baking, so always test for a successful result.

Testing sponges

Gently press the centre – it should feel springy. If your fingers leave a depression, the cake needs to be returned to the oven. Retest every 5 minutes. Alternatively, a skewer inserted into the centre should come out clean. If it is a whisked sponge just do the finger test, because skewering the cake can cause it to sink. Another test for a whisked sponge is that it should just be shrinking away from the sides of the tin.

Testing fruit cakes

Insert a skewer into the centre – if it comes out clean, the cake is ready. If any mixture sticks to the skewer, the cake is not done. Put it back into the oven for 5–10 minutes more, then test again with a clean skewer.

4 Splitting and filling

Sponge cakes can be split and filled with jam (jelly),
cream or buttercream. Icings or frostings complete
a special-occasion cake and are especially good over
homemade almond paste.

1 Leave the cake to cool completely before splitting.
Use a knife with a shallow thin blade, such as a bread
knife, ham knife, or carving knife. Cut a notch from
top to bottom on one side so you know where to line
the pieces up.

2 Cut midway between top and bottom, about
30% of the way through the cake. Turn the cake while
cutting, taking care to keep the blade parallel with
the base, until you have cut all the way around.

3 Cut through the central core and lift off the top of
the cake.

4 Warm the filling slightly to make it easier to
spread, then spread on top of the base, stopping
1cm/½in from the edge. Add the top layer of cake.

Victoria Sponge

Cuts into 10 slices

Preparation time: 20 minutes
Cooking time: about 25 minutes,
plus cooling

175g/6oz/1½ sticks unsalted
    butter at room temperature,
    plus extra to grease
175g/6oz/¾ cup golden caster
    sugar
3 medium (US large) eggs
175g/6oz/1¼ cups self-raising
    (self-rising) flour, sifted
3–4 tbsp jam (jelly)
A little icing (confectioners') sugar
    to dust

PER SLICE: 445 cals; 21g fat (of which 11g
saturates); 30g carbohydrate; 0.8g salt

1   Grease two 18cm/7in sandwich tins (pans) and base-line **1**
with greaseproof (wax) paper. Preheat the oven to 190°C (170°C fan
oven)/375°F/Gas mark 5.

2   Put the butter and caster sugar into a large bowl and, using a hand-
held electric whisk, beat together until pale and fluffy **2**. Add the eggs,
one at a time, beating well after each addition and adding a spoonful of
flour to the mixture if it looks as if it's about to curdle. Using a large metal
spoon, fold in the remaining flour.

3   Divide the mixture evenly between the prepared tins and level the
surface with a palette knife. Bake in the centre of the oven for 20–25
minutes until the cakes are well risen and spring back when lightly
pressed in the centre **3**. Loosen the edges with a palette knife and leave
in the tins for 5 minutes.

4   Turn out, remove the lining paper and leave to cool on a wire rack.
Sandwich the two cakes together with jam (jelly) **4** and dust icing
(confectioners') sugar over the top. Slice and serve.

To store

Store in an airtight container. It will keep for up to three days. If stored in
the fridge it will keep for up to one week.

Chocolate Victoria Sandwich

Cuts into 8 slices

Preparation time: 20 minutes
Cooking time: 20 minutes, plus cooling

175g/6oz/1½ sticks unsalted
    butter at room temperature,
    plus extra to grease
3 tbsp cocoa powder
175g/6oz/¾ cup golden caster
    sugar
3 medium eggs (US large), beaten
160g/5½oz/1 heaping cup self-
    raising (self-rising) flour, sifted
Golden caster sugar to dredge

Chocolate buttercream filling:

1 tbsp cocoa powder
75g/3oz/¾ stick unsalted butter,
    softened
175g/6oz/1⅓ cups icing
    (confectioners') sugar, sifted
A few drops of vanilla extract
1–2 tbsp milk or water

PER SLICE: 520 cals; 30g fat (of which 19g saturates); 62g carbohydrate; 1g salt

1   Preheat the oven to 190°C (170°C fan oven)/375°F/Gas mark 5. Grease two 18cm/7in sandwich tins (pans) and base-line **1** with greaseproof (wax) paper or baking parchment. Blend the cocoa powder with 3 tbsp hot water to make a smooth paste, then leave to cool.

2   Using a freestanding mixer or hand-held electric whisk, cream the butter and sugar together until pale and fluffy **2** . Add the cooled cocoa mixture and beat until evenly blended.

3   Add the beaten eggs, a little at a time, beating well after each addition. Using a metal spoon or large spatula, fold in half the flour, then carefully fold in the rest. Divide the mixture evenly between the tins and level the surface.

4   Bake both cakes on the middle shelf of the oven for about 20 minutes until well risen, springy to the touch and beginning to shrink away from the sides of the tins **3** . Cool in the tins for 5 minutes, then turn out on to a wire rack and leave to cool completely.

5   To make the chocolate buttercream, blend the cocoa powder with 3 tbsp boiling water and set aside to cool. Put the butter into a bowl and beat with a wooden spoon until light and fluffy. Gradually stir in the icing (confectioners') sugar. Add the blended cocoa, vanilla extract and milk or water and beat well until light and smooth.

6   When the cakes are cool, sandwich them together **4** with the chocolate buttercream and sprinkle the top with caster sugar.

To store

Store in an airtight container in a cool place. It will keep well for up to one week.

Rich Fruit Cake

Cuts into 16 slices

Preparation Time: 30 minutes
Cooking time: 2½ hours, plus cooling

175g/6oz/1½ sticks unsalted
    butter, cubed, plus extra
    to grease
1kg /2¼lb/6⅔ cups mixed
    dried fruit
100g/3½oz/½ cup ready-to-eat
    dried prunes, roughly chopped
50g/2oz/⅓ cup ready-to-eat dried
    figs, roughly chopped
100g/3½oz/1 cup dried
    cranberries
2 balls preserved stem ginger
    in syrup, grated and syrup
    reserved
Grated zest and juice of 1 orange
175ml/6fl oz/¾ cup brandy
2 splashes Angostura bitters
175g /6oz/1 cup dark muscovado
    (brown) sugar
200g/7oz/1⅓ cups self-raising
    (self-rising) flour
½ tsp ground cinnamon
½ tsp freshly grated nutmeg
½ tsp ground cloves
4 medium eggs (US large), beaten

PER SLICE: 277 cals; 11g fat (of which 6g saturates); 38g carbohydrate; 0.2g salt

1 Preheat the oven to 150°C (130°C fan oven)/300°F/Gas mark 2. Grease a 20.5cm/8in round, deep cake tin (pan) and line the base and sides **1** with greaseproof (wax) paper.

2 Put all the dried fruit into a very large pan and add the ginger, 1 tbsp reserved ginger syrup, the orange zest and juice, brandy and Angostura bitters. Bring to the boil, then simmer for 5 minutes. Add the butter and sugar and heat gently to melt. Stir occasionally until the sugar dissolves. Take the pan off the heat and leave to cool for a couple of minutes.

3 Add the flour, spices and beaten eggs and mix well **2**. Pour the mixture into the prepared tin and level the surface. Wrap the outside of the tin in brown paper and secure with string to protect the cake during cooking. Bake for 2–2½ hours – cover with greaseproof paper after about 1½ hours – until the cake is firm to the touch and a skewer inserted into the centre comes out clean **3**.

4 Cool in the tin for 2–3 hours, then remove from the tin, leaving the greaseproof paper on, transfer to a wire rack and leave to cool completely. Wrap the cake in a layer of cling film (plastic wrap), then in foil.

To store

Store in an airtight container. It will keep for up to three months. If you like, after the cake has matured for two weeks, prick it all over with a metal skewer and sprinkle with 1 tbsp brandy. Leave to soak in, then rewrap and store as before.

Quantities and sizes for rich fruit cakes

The ingredients required to fill different sizes of cake tin (pan), round or square. When baking large cakes, 25.5cm/10in and upwards, it is advisable to reduce the oven to 130°C (110°C fan oven)/250°F/Gas mark 1 after two-thirds of the cooking time. The amounts of almond paste quoted in this chart will give a thin covering. The quantities of royal icing should be enough for two coats. If using ready-to-roll fondant icing, use the quantities suggested for royal icing as a rough guide.

Cake tin size							
12.5cm/5in square	15cm/6in square	18cm/7in square	20.5cm/8in square	23cm/9in square	25.5cm/10in square	28cm/11in square	30.5cm/12in square
15cm/6in round	18cm/7in round	20.5cm/8in round	23cm/9in round	25.5cm/10in round	28cm/11in round	30.5cm/12in round	33cm/13in round
Currants							
225g/8oz	350g/12oz	450g/1lb	625g/1lb 6oz	775g/1lb 12oz	1.1kg/2lb 8oz	1.5kg/3lb 4oz	1.7kg/3lb 8oz
Sultanas (golden raisins)							
100g/3½oz	125g/4½oz	200g/7oz	225g/8oz	375g/13oz	400g/14oz	525g/1lb 3oz	625g/1lb 6oz
Raisins							
100g/3½oz	125g/4½oz	200g/7oz	225g/8oz	375g/13oz	400g/14oz	525g/1lb 3oz	625g/1lb 6oz
Glacé cherries							
50g/2oz	75g/3oz	150g/5oz	175g/6oz	250g/9oz	275g/10oz	350g/12oz	425g/15oz
Mixed peel							
25g/1oz	50g/2oz	75g/3oz	100g/3½oz	150g/5oz	200g/7oz	250g/9oz	275g/10oz
Flaked almonds							
25g/1oz	50g/2oz	75g/3oz	100g/3½oz	150g/5oz	200g/7oz	250g/9oz	275g/10oz
Lemon zest, grated							
a little	a little	a litle	¼ lemon	¼ lemon	½ lemon	½ lemon	1 lemon
Brandy							
1 tbsp	1 tbsp	1–2 tbsp	2 tbsp	2–3 tbsp	3 tbsp	4 tbsp	6 tbsp
Soft unsalted butter							
150g/5oz	175g/6oz	275g/10oz	350g/12oz	500g/1lb 2oz	600g/1lb 5oz	800g/1lb 12oz	950g/2lb 2oz
Plain (all-purpose) flour							
175g/6oz	215g/7½oz	350g/12oz	400g/14oz	600g/1lb 5oz	700g/1lb 8oz	825g/1lb 13oz	1kg/2lb 4oz
Mixed spice							
¼ tsp	½ tsp	½ tsp	1 tsp	1 tsp	2 tsp	2½ tsp	2½ tsp
Cinnamon							
¼ tsp	½ tsp	½ tsp	1 tsp	1 tsp	2 tsp	2½ tsp	2½ tsp
Soft brown sugar							
150g/5oz	175g/6oz	275g/10oz	350g/12oz	500g/1lb 2oz	600g/1lb 5oz	800g/1lb 12oz	950g/2lb 2oz
Medium eggs (US large) beaten							
2½	3	5	6	9	11	14	17
Baking time (approx.)							
2½–3 hours	3–3½ hours	3½ hours	4 hours	4½ hours	6 hours	6–6½ hours	6½ hours
Weight when cooked							
1.1kg/2½lb	1.5kg/3¼lb	2.1kg/4¾lb	2.7kg/6lb	3.8kg/8½lb	4.8kg/10½lb	6.1kg/13½lb	7.4kg/16½lb

Carrot Cake

Cuts into 12 slices

Preparation time: 15 minutes
Cooking time: 40 minutes,
plus cooling

250ml/9fl oz sunflower oil, plus
    extra to grease
225g/8oz/1¼ cups light
    muscovado (brown) sugar
3 large (US extra-large) eggs
225g/8oz/1½ cups self-raising
    (self-rising) flour
Large pinch of salt
½ tsp each ground mixed spice,
    ground nutmeg and ground
    cinnamon
250g/9oz/5 cups carrots, peeled
    and coarsely grated

Frosting:

50g/2oz/½ stick butter, preferably
    unsalted, at room temperature
225g/8oz pack cream cheese
25g/1oz/2 tsp golden icing
    (confectioners') sugar
½ tsp vanilla extract
8 pecan halves, roughly chopped

PER SLICE: 383 cals; 32g fat (of which 10g
saturates); 24g carbohydrate; 0.3g salt

1   Preheat the oven to 180°C (160°C fan oven)/350°F/Gas mark 4. Grease two 18cm/7in sandwich tins (pans) and base-line **1** with greaseproof (wax) paper.

2   Using a hand-held electric whisk, whisk the oil and sugar together to combine, then whisk in the eggs, one at a time **2**.

3   Sift the flour, salt and spices together over the mixture, then gently fold in, using a large metal spoon. Tip the carrots into the bowl and fold in.

4   Divide the cake mixture between the prepared tins and bake for 30–40 minutes until golden and a skewer inserted into the centre comes out clean **3**. Remove from the oven and leave in the tins for 10 minutes, then turn out on to a wire rack and leave to cool completely.

5   To make the frosting, beat the butter and cream cheese together in a bowl until light and fluffy. Sift in the icing (confectioners') sugar, add the vanilla extract and beat well until smooth. Spread one-third of the frosting over one cake **7** and sandwich together **4** with the other cake. Spread the remaining frosting on top and sprinkle with the pecans.

To store

Store in an airtight container. Eat within two days. Alternatively, the cake will keep for up to one week in an airtight container if it is stored before the frosting is applied.

Madeira Cake

Cuts into 12 slices

Preparation time: 20 minutes
Cooking time: about 50 minutes,
plus cooling

175g/6oz/1½ sticks butter,
    softened, plus extra to grease
125g/4oz/heaping ¾ cup plain
    (all-purpose) flour
125g/4oz/¾ cup self-raising
    (self-rising) flour
175g/6oz/¾ cup golden
    caster sugar
1 tsp vanilla extract
3 large eggs (US extra-large),
    beaten
1–2 tbsp milk (optional)
2–3 thin slices citron peel

1   Preheat the oven to 180°C (160°C fan oven)/350°F/Gas mark 4. Grease and line **1** a deep 18cm/7in round cake tin (pan). Sift the plain (all-purpose) and self-raising (self-rising) flours together.
2   Cream the butter and sugar together in a bowl until pale and fluffy **2**, then beat in the vanilla extract. Add the eggs, a little at a time, beating well after each addition.
3   Using a metal spoon, fold in the sifted flours, adding a little milk if necessary to give a dropping consistency.
4   Spoon the mixture into the prepared tin and level the surface. Bake for 20 minutes. Lay the citron peel on the cake and bake for a further 30 minutes, or until a skewer inserted into the centre of the cake comes out clean **3**. Turn out on to a wire rack and leave to cool. This cake can be made up to one week in advance (store in an airtight tin) or frozen for up to one month.

Variation
Add the grated zest of 1 lemon at stage 2. Add the juice of the lemon instead of the milk at stage 3.

PER SLICE: 260 cals; 14g fat (of which 8g saturates); 31g carbohydrate; 0.4g salt

Quantities and sizes for Madeira cakes

The ingredients required to fill different sizes of cake tin (pan), whether round or square.

Cake tin (pan) size	15cm/6in square / 18cm/7in round	18cm/7in square / 20.5cm/8in round	20.5cm/8in square / 23cm/9in round	23cm/9in square / 25.5cm/10in round	25.5cm/10in square / 28cm/11in round	28cm/11in square / 30.5cm/12in round	30.5cm/12in square / 33cm/13in round
Plain (all-purpose) flour	125g/4oz	175g/6oz	225g/8oz	250g/9oz	275g/10oz	350g/12oz	450g/1lb
Self-raising (self-rising) flour	125g/4oz	175g/6oz	225g/8oz	250g/9oz	275g/10oz	350g/12oz	450g/1lb
Soft unsalted butter	175g/6oz	275g/10oz	400g/14oz	450g/1lb	500g/1lb 2oz	625g/1lb 6oz	725g/1lb 10oz
Caster sugar	175g/6oz	275g/10oz	400g/14oz	450g/1lb	500g/1lb 2oz	625g/1lb 6oz	725g/1lb 10oz
Medium eggs beaten	3	5	7	8	10	12	13
Lemon juice or milk	2 tbsp	3 tbsp	3½ tbsp	4 tbsp	4 ½ tbsp	5 tbsp	5½ tbsp
Baking time (approx.)	1¼–1½ hours	1 ½–1¾ hours	1¾–2 hours	1¾–2 hours	2–2¼ hours	2¼–2½ hours	2½–2¾ hours

Marble Cake

Cuts into 8 slices

Preparation time: 25 minutes
Cooking time: about 45 minutes,
plus cooling and setting

175g/6oz/1½ sticks unsalted
    butter, softened, plus extra
    to grease
175g/6oz/¾ cup caster sugar
3 medium (US large) eggs,
    lightly beaten
125g/4oz/heaping ¾ cup
    self-raising (self-rising) flour
1 tsp baking powder
50g/2oz/⅓ cup ground almonds
1 tbsp milk
2 tbsp cocoa powder, sifted

To ice:
200g/7oz plain dark (semi-sweet)
    chocolate
75g/3oz/¾ stick butter

PER SLICE: 579 cals; 40g fat (of which 22g
saturates); 52g carbohydrate; 1g salt

Note
Dragging a skewer through
two contrasting-coloured cake
mixes is the secret to making a
professional-looking marble cake.

1   Preheat the oven to 190°C (170°C fan oven)/375°F/Gas mark 5. Grease a 900g/2lb loaf tin (pan) and line **1** with greaseproof (wax) paper, then grease the paper lightly.

2   Using a hand-held electric whisk, cream the butter and sugar together **2** until pale and fluffy. Gradually add the eggs, beating well after each addition.

3   Sift the flour and baking powder into the bowl, then add the ground almonds and milk. Using a large metal spoon, fold everything together. Spoon half the mixture into a clean bowl and fold through the sifted cocoa powder.

4   Spoon a dollop of each mixture alternately into the prepared tin until you have used up both mixtures. Bang the base of the tin once on a surface to level and remove any air bubbles. Draw a skewer backwards and forwards through the mixture a few times to create a marbled effect. Bake for 45 minutes to 1 hour until a skewer inserted into the centre comes out clean **3**.

5   Leave the cake to cool for 15 minutes in the tin, then lift out and cool completely on a wire rack.

6   To ice, melt the chocolate and butter together gently in a pan. Put the cake (without greaseproof paper) on a wire rack. Pour the chocolate over and leave to set before serving.

Cupcakes

Makes 18

Preparation time: 20 minutes
Cooking time: 10–15 minutes,
plus cooling and setting

125g/4oz/heaping ¾ cup self-
　　raising (self-rising) flour, sifted
1 tsp baking powder
125g/4oz/½ cup caster sugar
125g/4oz/1 stick unsalted butter,
　　very soft
2 medium (US large) eggs
1 tbsp milk

Icing and decoration:
225g/8oz/1¾ cups icing
　　(confectioners') sugar, sifted
Assorted food colourings
　　(optional)
Sweets (candies), sprinkles or
　　coloured sugar

PER CAKE: 160 cals; 6g fat (of which 4g
saturates); 26g carbohydrate; 0.2g salt

To freeze, complete the
recipe to the end of step 3.
Open-freeze, then wrap the
cakes and freeze. To use,
thaw for about 1 hour, then
complete the recipe.

1　Preheat the oven to 200°C (180°C fan oven)/400°F/Gas mark 6. Put paper cases (liners) into 18 of the holes in two cupcake tins (pans).
2　Put the flour, baking powder, sugar, butter, eggs and milk into a mixing bowl and beat **1** with a hand-held electric whisk for 2 minutes or until the mixture is pale and very soft. Half-fill each paper case with the mixture.
3　Bake for 10–15 minutes until golden brown. Transfer to a wire rack and leave to cool completely.
4　Put the icing (confectioners') sugar into a bowl and gradually blend in 2–3 tbsp warm water until the icing is fairly stiff, but spreadable. Add a couple of drops of food colouring, if you like.
5　When the cakes are cold, spread the tops with the icing and decorate. Leave to set.

To store
Store in an airtight container. They will keep for 3–5 days.

Variation
Chocolate cupcakes: Replace 2 tbsp of the flour with the same amount of cocoa. Stir 50g/2oz chocolate drops, sultanas (golden raisins) or chopped apricots into the mix at the end of step 1. Complete the recipe.

Icing and Frosting Recipes

Glacé Icing

To make 225g/8oz, enough to cover 18 cupcakes, you will need: 225g/8oz/1¾ cups icing (confectioners') sugar, a few drops of vanilla or almond flavouring (optional), 2–3 tbsp boiling water, food colouring (optional).

1 Sift the sugar into a bowl. Add a few drops of flavouring, if you like.

2 Using a wooden spoon, gradually stir in enough water until the mixture is the consistency of thick cream. Beat until white and smooth and the icing is thick enough to coat the back of the spoon. Add colouring, if you like, and use immediately.

Variations

- **Orange or lemon:** Replace the water with strained orange or lemon juice.
- **Chocolate:** Sift 2 tsp cocoa powder with the icing (confectioners') sugar.
- **Colour:** Add a few drops of liquid food colouring, or use food colouring paste for a stronger colour.

Buttercream

To cover the top of a 20.5cm/8in cake, you will need: 75g/3oz/¾ stick unsalted butter, 175g/6oz/1⅓ cups icing (confectioners') sugar, sifted, a few drops of vanilla extract, 1–2 tbsp milk.

1 Soften the butter in a mixing bowl, then beat until light and fluffy.

2 Gradually stir in the remaining ingredients and beat until smooth.

Food colourings are available in liquid, paste or powder form. Add tiny amounts with the tip of a cocktail stick until the desired colour is achieved.

Variations

- **Citrus:** Replace the vanilla with a little grated orange, lemon or lime zest, and use some of the fruit's juice in place of the milk.
- **Chocolate:** Blend 1 tbsp cocoa powder with 2 tbsp boiling water. Cool, then add to the mixture in place of the milk.
- **Colour:** For a strong colour, use food colouring paste; liquid colouring gives a paler effect.

Easy Icing

To make 675g/1½lb, enough to cover a 20.5cm/8in almond paste-covered cake, you will need: 3 medium (US large) egg whites, 2 tbsp lemon juice, 2 tsp glycerine, 675g/1½lb/5½ cups icing (confectioners') sugar, sifted.

1 Put the egg whites into a large bowl and whisk until frothy. There should be a thin layer of bubbles over the top. Add the lemon juice, glycerine and 2 tbsp icing (confectioners') sugar and whisk until smooth.

2 Whisk in the rest of the sugar, a little at a time, until the mixture is smooth, thick and forming soft peaks.

3 Using a palette knife (metal spatula), smooth half the icing over the top and sides of the cake, then repeat with the remaining icing to cover. Run the knife around the sides to neaten, then use the tip to make peaks all over the top. Leave to dry in a cool place for at least 48 hours.

Fondant Icing

To make 500g/1lb 2oz, enough to cover the top and sides of an 18cm/7in round cake or 15cm/6in square cake, you will need: 500g/1lb 2oz/4 cups golden icing (confectioners') sugar, plus extra to dust, 1 medium (US large) egg white, 2 tbsp liquid glucose, warmed, 1 tsp vanilla extract.

Whiz the icing (confectioners') sugar in a food processor for 30 seconds, then add the egg white, glucose and vanilla extract and whiz for 2–3 minutes until the mixture forms a ball.

Almond Paste

To make 450g/1lb almond paste (marzipan), enough to cover the top and sides of an 18cm/7in round cake or 15cm/6in square cake, you will need: 225g/8oz/1½ cups ground almonds, 125g /4oz/½ cup golden caster sugar, 125g/4oz/1 cup sifted golden icing (confectioners') sugar, 1 large (US extra-large) egg, 2 tsp lemon juice, 1 tsp sherry, 1–2 drops vanilla extract.

1 Put the ground almonds and sugars into a bowl and stir to combine. In another bowl, whisk together the remaining ingredients, then add to the dry ingredients.

2 Stir well to mix, pounding gently to release some of the oil from the almonds. Knead with your hands until smooth, then cover until ready to use.

Quantity of almond paste needed

Weight	Square cake	Round cake
450g/1lb	12.5cm/5in	15cm/6in
550g/1¼lb	15cm/6in	18cm/7in
700g/1½lb	18cm/7in	20.5cm/8in
800g/1¾lb	20.5cm/8in	23cm/9in
1kg/2¼lb	23cm/9in	25.5cm/10in
1.1kg 2½lb	25.5cm/10in	28cm/11in
1.25kg/2¾lb	28cm/11in	30.5cm/12in
1.6kg/3½lb	30.5cm/12in	33cm/13in

Apricot Glaze

To make 450g/1lb, you will need: 450g/1lb apricot jam (jelly), 2 tbsp water

1 Put the jam (jelly) and water into a saucepan and heat gently, stirring occasionally, until melted. Boil the jam rapidly for 1 minute, then strain through a sieve.

2 Using a wooden spoon, rub through as much fruit as possible. Discard the skins left in the sieve.

3 Pour the glaze into a clean, hot jar, then seal with a clean lid and cool, Store in the fridge for up to two months. You only need 3–4 tbsp apricot glaze for a 23cm/9in cake, so this quantity will glaze 6–7 cakes.

Royal Icing

This can also be bought in packs from supermarkets. Simply add water or egg white to use. To make 450g/1lb, enough to cover the top and sides of a 20.5cm/8in cake, you will need: 2 medium (US large) egg whites, ¼ tsp lemon juice, 450g/1lb/3½ cups icing (confectioners') sugar, sifted, 1 tsp glycerine.

1 Put the egg whites and lemon juice into a clean bowl. Stir to break up the egg whites. Add sufficient icing (confectioners') sugar to mix to the consistency of unwhipped cream. Continue mixing and adding small quantities of icing sugar until the desired consistency is reached, mixing well and gently beating after each addition. The icing should be smooth, glossy and light, almost like a cold meringue in texture, but not aerated. Do not add the icing sugar too quickly or it will produce a dull heavy icing. Stir in the glycerine until well blended. (Alternatively, for large quantities of royal icing, use a food mixer on the lowest speed, following the same instructions as before.)

2 Allow the icing to settle before using it; cover the surface with a piece of damp cling film (plastic wrap) and seal well, excluding all the air.

3 Stir the icing thoroughly before use to disperse any air bubbles, then adjust the consistency if necessary by adding more sifted icing sugar.

If you wish to avoid using raw egg to bind the almond paste, mix the other liquid ingredients with a little water instead.

Royal icing consistency

The skill of royal icing and the quality of the result is dependent on using the correct consistency.

Cake-covering consistency

Stir the icing well with a wooden spoon then lift the spoon out of the icing. The icing on the spoon should form a fine point that just curves over at the end – this stage is known as 'soft peak'. This consistency spreads smoothly and evenly and creates a flat finish, or can be pulled up into sharp or soft peaks.

Piping consistency

Stir the icing well with a wooden spoon then lift the spoon out of the icing. The icing on the spoon should form a fine, sharp point – this stage is known as 'sharp peak'. It will flow easily for piping and will retain the definite shape of the piping nozzle (tip) used. When piping from a very fine writing nozzle the icing will need to be made slighly softer to avoid aching wrists.

Run-out decoration consistency

Omit the glycerine when making royal icing for run-outs so that they dry hard and are easy to handle without breakages. A 'medium peak' consistency is used to pipe outlines to retain the shape of the run-out; icing the consistency of thick cream is used to fill in the shapes. This icing consistency flows with the help of a fine brush to fill in the run-outs, but holds a rounded shape within the piped lines.

Quantity of royal icing needed

Weight	Square cake	Round cake
450g/1lb	12.5cm/5in	15cm/6in
700g/1½lb	15cm/6in	18cm/7in
900g/2lb	18cm/7in	20.5cm/8in
1.1kg/2½lb	20.5cm/8in	23cm/9in
1.4kg/3lb	23cm/9in	25.5cm/10in
1.6kg/3½lb	25.5cm/10in	28cm/11in
1.8kg/4lb	28cm/11in	30.5cm/12in
2kg/4½lb	30.5cm/12in	33cm/13in

Chocolate Ganache

Use ganache at room temperature as a smooth coating for special cakes, or chill it lightly until thickened and use to fill meringues, choux buns or sandwich cakes. To make 225g/8oz, enough to cover an 18cm/7in round cake, you will need: 225g/8oz good-quality plain dark (semi-sweet) chocolate (with 60–70% cocoa solids), chopped into small pieces, 250ml/9fl oz double (heavy) cream.

1 Put the chocolate into a medium heatproof bowl. Pour the cream into a small heavy-based pan and bring to the boil.

2 Immediately pour the cream onto the chocolate and stir gently in one direction until the chocolate has melted and the mixture is smooth. Set aside to cool for 5 minutes.

3 Whisk the ganache until it begins to hold its shape. Used at room temperature, the mixture should be the consistency of softened butter.

Variations

- **Milk or single cream (half-and-half):** Substitute in whole or in part for the water.
- **Coffee:** Stir in 1 tsp instant coffee or a shot of espresso when melting the chocolate.
- **Spices:** Add a pinch of ground cinnamon, crushed cardamom seeds or freshly grated nutmeg to the melting chocolate.
- **Vanilla extract:** Stir in ¼ tsp vanilla when melting the chocolate.
- **Rum, whisky or Cognac:** Stir in about 1 tsp alcohol when melting the chocolate.
- **Butter:** Stir in 25g/1oz/¼ stick towards the end of heating.

Vanilla Frosting

To make about 175g/6oz, enough to cover the top and sides of an 18cm/7in cake, you will need: 150g/5oz/1¼ cups icing (confectioners') sugar, 5 tsp vegetable oil, 1 tbsp milk, a few drops of vanilla extract.

Sift the icing (confectioners') sugar into a bowl and, using a wooden spoon, beat in the oil, milk and vanilla extract until smooth.

Coffee Fudge Frosting

To make 400g/14oz, enough to cover the top and sides of a 20.5cm/8in cake, you will need: 50g/2oz/½ stick unsalted butter, 125g/4oz/¾ cup light muscovado (brown) sugar, 2 tbsp single cream (half-and-half) or milk, 1 tbsp coffee granules, 200g/7oz/1½ cups golden icing (confectioners') sugar, sifted.

1 Put the butter, muscovado (brown) sugar and cream (half-and-half) or milk into a pan. Dissolve the coffee in 2 tbsp boiling water and add to the pan. Heat gently until the sugar dissolves, then bring to the boil and boil briskly for 3 minutes.

2 Remove from the heat and gradually stir in the icing (confectioners') sugar. Beat well with a wooden spoon for 1 minute until smooth.

3 Use the frosting immediately, spreading it over the cake with a wet palette knife, or dilute with a little water to use as a smooth coating.

Variation

Chocolate fudge frosting: Omit the coffee. Add 75g/3oz plain (semi-sweet) chocolate, in pieces, to the pan with the butter at the beginning of step 1.

American Frosting

To make 225g/8oz, enough to cover the top and sides of a 20.5cm/8in cake, you will need: 1 large (US extra-large) egg white, 225g/8oz/1 cup golden caster or granulated sugar, pinch of cream of tartar.

1 Whisk the egg white in a clean bowl until stiff. Put the sugar, 4 tbsp water and the cream of tartar into a heavy-based pan. Heat gently, stirring, until the sugar has dissolved. Bring to the boil, without stirring, and boil until the sugar syrup registers 115°C/230°F on a sugar thermometer.

2 Remove from the heat and, as soon as the bubbles subside, pour the syrup on to the egg white in a thin stream, whisking constantly until thick and white. Leave to cool slightly.

3 When the frosting begins to turn dull around the edges and is almost cold, pour quickly over the cake and spread evenly with a palette knife.

Seven-minute Frosting

To make about 175g/6oz, enough to cover the top and sides of an 18cm/7in cake, you will need: 1 medium (US large) egg white, 175g/6oz/¾ cup caster sugar, 2 tbsp water, pinch of salt, pinch of cream of tartar.

1 Put all the ingredients into a heatproof bowl and whisk lightly using an electric or hand whisk.

2 Put the bowl over a pan of hot water, making sure the base of the bowl doesn't touch the water, and heat, whisking continuously, until the mixture thickens sufficiently to stand in peaks. This will take about 7 minutes.

3 Pour the frosting over the top of the cake and spread with a palette knife.

Covering Cakes

There are lots of options for covering cakes, depending on the finish you require. Each icing or frosting has its own characteristic texture, flavour, colour and consistency; some can be poured over a cake for a perfectly smooth finish, others need to be spread or swirled for texture.

5 Buttercream icing

Buttercream can be piped or spread on to cakes. Fill your cake first, if needed, before icing. Always stir the buttercream well before spreading or piping to ensure that it has a smooth, soft consistency.

To pipe, choose your nozzle (tip) and fill the piping bag (decorating bag) with buttercream. After some practice, simply pipe on to your cake, squeezing with an even pressure. Allow to harden.

To spread, use a palette knife (metal spatula) to spread buttercream evenly over the top of your cake, paddling it backward and forward to eliminate any air bubbles. Have  a jug of hot water near to dip the palette knife into as you spread the icing, so that it doesn't stick to the knife and pull up the crumb surface. Move the cake (on its cake board) to a turntable and use a palette knife to spread icing over the sides, paddling as you go. Swirl the top and sides into a pattern. Leave to set.

Coating the sides of a cake with nuts adds flavour, crunch and visual appeal. Your cake needs to have been just iced with buttercream or frosting (so it is still sticky). Put the iced  cake on a large sheet of greaseproof paper. Working in sections, scatter nuts around the cake and use the paper to ease the nuts on to the cake – work slowly so that the nuts are not catapulted on to the top of the cake. Fill in any gaps by pressing the nuts on to the cake using your hands.

> To cover a cake with a basic icing such as buttercream or glacé, first make sure your icing is well beaten, smooth and soft in texture, so that it does not pull up the surface crumbs of the cake as you spread it. Practise by spreading some on a board first.

6 Glacé icing

Glacé icing gives an even surface and is popular with children and adults alike. It takes a fair amount of time to dry so factor this in.

 To glacé ice the top of a cake, make a wide double thickness collar of greaseproof (wax) paper and wrap tightly around the cake, so that it extends about 5cm/2in above the top. Fix in place with a paper clip. Pour the icing onto the cake and spread almost to the collar. Leave to harden before removing the collar.

 To glacé ice the top and sides pour the icing onto the centre of the cake and, using a palette knife (metal spatula), spread it right to the edges. Allow the icing to run down the sides evenly (with the help of your palette knife, if needed). Fill in any spaces with surplus icing from the bowl or from the baking sheet (taking care not to include crumbs). Clean the base.

7 Frosting

Using frosting you can achieve both satin-smooth and textured finishes. Frostings are often used while warm.

1 Make sure the frosting is the correct consistency – thick enough to coat the back of a spoon. If it is too thick, the bowl will need to be placed over hot water or the frosting may be thinned with a little water. If the frosting is too slack, leave it to cool and thicken slightly before using.

2 Pour all the frosting over the top of the cake and allow it to fall over the sides, gently tapping the cake to encourage it to flow – don't be tempted to use a knife, which would leave marks on the surface. When the frosting has stopped falling, neaten the bottom edge and leave to dry.

8 Covering with almond paste for royal icing

1 Trim the top of the cake level if necessary then turn the cake over to give a flat surface to work on. Place on a cake board at least 5cm/2in larger than the cake. Brush the cake with warmed apricot glaze (see page 33).

2 Dust the work surface with sifted icing (confectioners') sugar. Knead half the specified almond paste (see quantity chart, page 33), and roll out to a thickness of 5mm/¼in to roughly match the size of the cake. Make sure the almond paste is not sticking to the surface, then invert the cake onto the centre. Using a small knife, trim off excess almond paste to within 1cm/½in of the cake.

Once you have covered the cake with almond pastepiping, leave the cake in a cool, dry place to dry out for at least 24 hours before covering with ready-to-roll icing or for at least two days before applying royal icing. Homemade almond paste takes a little longer to dry out than the ready-made variety.

3 Using a palette knife, push the paste level with the sides of the cake until all the edges are neat. Invert the cake (almond paste up) and put on to a cake board about 5cm/2in larger than the cake.

4 Cut a piece of string the height as the cake plus almond paste topping, and another to fit around the diameter. Roll out the remaining almond paste to a thickness of 5mm/¼in and use the string as a guide to trim it to size. Roll up the almond paste strip loosely. Place one end against the side of the cake and unroll the strip around the cake to cover it. Use a palette knife to smooth over the sides and joins.

9 Covering with almond paste for sugarpaste

1 Follow step 1 as for a royal iced cake. Knead the specified almond paste quantity for your cake until smooth, then roll out to 5mm/¼in thickness until the almond paste is large enough to cover the top and sides of the cake, allowing about 5–7.5cm/2–3in extra all the way round.

2 Roll the almond paste loosely around the rolling pin. Starting from one side of the cake, carefully unroll the almond paste onto the cake. Working from the centre, carefully smooth the almond paste over the top, ensuring there are no trapped air pockets, then smooth down the sides. Lift the edges slightly to allow the almond paste to be eased in to fit the base of the cake without stretching or tearing the top edge. Using a small knife, trim off excess almond paste from the base. Using clean, dry hands or a cake smoother, gently rub the cake in circular movements to give the almond paste a glossy, rounded finish.

10 Royal icing

This method gives crisp, neat edges and a sparkling white finish. If you are less bothered about the finish, ice the entire cake in one go. Always cover royal icing with a damp piece of cling film (plastic wrap) when not using it to prevent it drying out.

> **Smoothing imperfections**
>
> Use fine sandpaper to buff down any imperfections (such as the 'pull off' mark) in the dry layers as you go along.

Square cake

1 Make a quantity of royal icing to soft peak consistency (see page 34), then lay a damp piece of cling film in the bowl, touching the icing, to prevent it drying out. The almond pasted (and dried) cake should be on a cake board. Have ready a palette knife (metal spatula), straight edge and a side scraper.

2 Using the palette knife, apply royal icing to the top of the cake to cover the surface evenly. Paddle back and forth in lines to help eliminate air bubbles. Smooth as best as possible.

3 Holding each end of the straight edge place it at the far side of the cake, just resting on the icing, then in one continuous movement pull across the top of the cake towards you. If the icing is not smooth enough, repeat using a clean straight edge. If the icing becomes thin, apply more before using the straight edge. If you don't have a straight edge, the edge of a large palette knife will work.

4 Use a clean palette knife to scrape any icing off the edges. Leave the top layer to dry for about 2 hours or overnight in a warm, dry place.

5 Put the cake on a turntable and, using a palette knife (a small one with a cranked handle is best), smoothly spread royal icing to cover one side evenly. Paddle the icing back and forth to eliminate air bubbles. Remove excess icing from the dry icing on top of the cake and from both corners, then pull a side scraper across the side to even the edge up. Repeat if not neat enough, adding more icing as necessary. Ice the opposite side and leave to dry for at least 2 hours.

6 Royal ice the remaining two sides of the cake as before. Trim away excess icing from the top edge and corners and leave to dry overnight.

7 Apply 1–3 further thin layers of royal icing until the icing is smooth and flat. For a really smooth finish use icing with a slightly softer consistency for the final coating. Ice the cake board, if needed, using a small palette knife and a side scraper.

Round cake

1 Holding each end of the straight edge place it at the far side of the cake, just resting on the icing, then in one continuous movement pull across the top of the cake towards you. If the icing is not smooth enough, repeat using a clean straight edge. If the icing becomes thin, apply more before using the straight edge. Remove any excess icing, then leave the top layer to dry for about 2 hours or overnight in a warm, dry place.

2 Put the cake on a turntable and use a palette knife (metal spatula) to spread royal icing around the side evenly, paddling it back and forward to eliminate air bubbles. Hold a cake scraper against the icing, resting the base of it on a cake board. With your other hand hold the edge of the cake board and turntable. Slowly turn the turntable while at the same time holding the side scraper against the icing, pulling it towards you in the opposite direction of the turning, to smooth the surface. Once you have gone round the cake, gradually pull off the side scraper (it will leave a 'pull off' mark). Neaten the top edge, then leave the cake to dry.

3 Repeat the process to cover the cake with 1–3 further thin layers of royal icing, using a slightly softer consistency for the final layer to give a smooth and sparkling finish. Ice the cake board, if needed, using a small palette knife and a side scraper.

Fondant icing

Also known as ready-to-roll icing or sugarpaste (gumpaste), this is pliable and can be used to cover cakes or moulded into shapes for decoration. Blocks of ready-to-roll icing are available in a variety of colours from supermarkets and cake decorating shops, or you can colour white icing to your desired shade. Simply brush your almond pasted cake with some brandy or boiled and cooled water and ease the icing over the cake as detailed right.

11 Covering a cake with sugarpaste

Always wear a white cotton apron over a white shirt or t-shirt when working with sugarpaste (gumpaste), so that coloured fabric particles don't fall into the icing. A 450g/1lb pack will cover an 18cm/7in cake. Wrap unused icing in cling film (plastic wrap) to stop it drying out and store in a cool, dry place.

Round cake

1   Dust the work surface and rolling pin with sifted icing (confectioners') sugar. Knead the icing until pliable, then roll out into a round or square 5–7.5cm/2–3in larger than the cake all round. Lift the icing on top of the cake and allow it to drape over the edges.

2   Dust your hands with sifted icing sugar and press the icing on to the sides of the cake, easing it down to the board.

3   Using a sharp knife, trim off the excess icing at the base to neaten. Reserve the trimmings to make decorations if required.

4   Using your fingers dusted with a little sifted icing (confectioners') sugar, gently rub the surface in a circular movement to buff the icing and make it completely smooth.

Shaped cake

1   Put the almond pasted cake on its matching cake board on a turntable. Brush the surface evenly with a little brandy or cooled boiled water. When covering a sponge cake with sugarpaste, spread with a thin layer of apricot jam (jelly) or buttercream first instead of a layer of almond paste.

2   Dust the work surface and the rolling pin with a little sifted icing (confectioners') sugar. Roll out the sugarpaste (gumpaste) to a 5mm/¼in thickness to match the shape of the cake and large enough to cover the top and sides with a little extra all round.

3   Gently roll the sugarpaste on to the rolling pin, then lift over the cake. Starting at one side, unroll the sugarpaste, allowing it to cover the cake loosely. With clean, dry hands, lightly smooth the sugarpaste over the top, excluding any trapped air bubbles. Ease gently on to the sides of the cake so that the excess sugarpaste is on the board.

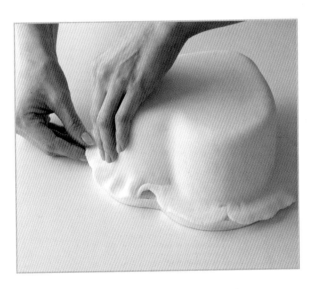

4   Using a small knife, trim off the excess sugarpaste at the base of the cake. With your hands or a cake smoother, gently smooth the surface and side of the cake in circular movements to ensure a smooth and glossy finish. Leave to harden overnight.

12 Covering cake boards

If you like the appearance of a cake board covered with sugarpaste (gumpaste), there are two ways to go about this.

1   Brush the board with water, then cover with sugarpaste and leave to dry. Place the almond pasted cake on the board, then apply the icing to the cake.

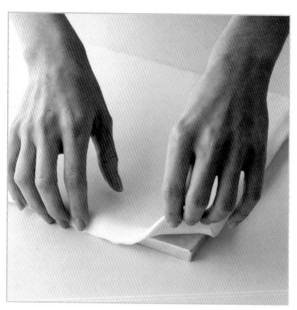

2   Alternatively, place the cake on the board. Roll out the sugarpaste large enough to cover the entire cake as well as the visible board and its sides. Lightly brush the cake and board with brandy or cooled boiled water. Place the sugarpaste over the cake and board, moulding it to fit around the cake, then trim around the board to neaten.

13 Icing and frosting cupcakes

The icing on cupcakes is almost as important as the cake underneath. Icing helps keep the cake softer for longer (as long as the cakes are kept in their paper cases/liners) and allows you to theme and decorate your cupcakes as desired.

Filling cupcakes

Before icing it, you can fill your cupcake with extra icing, buttercream or smooth jam (jelly). Fit a piping (decorating) bag with a plain nozzle (tip) (not too fine), half-fill with the chosen filling and push the nozzle down through the top into the centre of the un-iced cake (alternatively, hollow out some of the cake with a small knife first). Squeeze in some mixture, then ice as normal. It's worth cutting your first filled cake in half vertically to check how much filling you have managed to get into it.

Spreading

Start by gently brushing the top of the cooled cupcake with your finger or a brush to remove crumbs. Dollop a generous amount of buttercream or frosting onto the cake (it takes more than you might think) and gently spread the icing to the sides of the cake with a palette or butter knife for a smooth look. Alternatively, push the icing into a swirl or points with a spatula or knife.

Flooding cupcakes

Use a little less cake mixture when baking the cupcakes, so that when baked they don't quite reach the top of their cases. Spoon some glacé icing on top of the cooled cakes so that it floods out to the sides of the case. Decorate with feathering **27** , sprinkles, dragees, gold leaf or other decorations as desired.

Covering with sugarpaste

This works best if the cupcakes are flat – if they have peaked during baking, then trim to flatten. Roll out some sugarpaste (gumpaste) in the desired colour, to a thickness of 5mm/¼in. Measure the top of the cupcakes, then cut out circles of sugarpaste to match. Spread a thin layer of buttercream over the cupcake, then add the sugarpaste circle. If you don't want to completely cover the tops with sugarpaste, cut out smaller shapes of the sugarpaste – hearts always look nice – and leave to dry completely on greaseproof (wax) paper or baking parchment. Position on buttercreamed cupcakes (the decorations should be stiff enough to stand up).

Piping icing on to cupcakes

Many cupcake bakeries have developed a signature swirl of buttercream icing – practise and soon you'll have your own. Half-fill a piping (decorating) bag with buttercream or frosting and hold the bag vertically as you pipe, squeezing gently from the top. Choose from the shapes below, or use your imagination.

Swirl – fit a piping (decorating) bag with a large star or plain nozzle (tip). Starting from an outside edge, pipe an ever-decreasing circle onto the cupcake, slightly lifting the piping bag as you go. End with a point in the middle by sharply pulling away the piping bag.

Rosettes or blobs – the size of a rosette or blob depends on the nozzle used and the pressure applied to the piping (decorating) bag. Fit the bag with a plain nozzle (for blobs) or a star (for rosettes). Holding the piping bag upright just above the surface, squeeze out icing onto the cake (keeping the nozzle still). Pull up sharply to break the icing. Repeat to cover the cake surface with rosettes or blobs – it's easiest working in ever-decreasing circles.

Ribbons

Ribbons are invaluable when decorating any type of celebration or everyday cake. They are the one non-edible decoration that transforms the simplest cake into something quite special. There are, of course, many types of ribbon to choose from. If you are planning a very special cake, it is worth taking a trip to a haberdashery (sewing notion) or specialist ribbon shop to find the ideal ribbon for the occasion. The most popular ribbon is the double-faced polyester satin, which comes in a huge range of widths and colours. It is most useful for making bows, loops and tails for cake decorations and flower sprays. It is also used to band the edges of cake boards and to fit around the sides of cakes.

Securing ribbons to cake boards

Choose a ribbon that's the same width as your cake board, then cut it to length. Wrap tightly around the sides of the board, then secure in place with a stainless steel pin.

14 Ribbon bows

These are perfect for tying around the base of celebrations cakes, most notably Christmas cakes. Use a wide ribbon to create a big impact. Small bows, made with narrow ribbon, can be attached to the side or top of a celebration cake or cake board to enhance a border design or edging. Try making bows with long tail ends and curling them gently by pulling the ends over the cutting blade of a pair of scissors (hold one section of ribbon to the blade with your thumb, and pull it through, keeping the pressure tight). This technique looks pretty cascading over the edge of a cake.

15 Adding ribbon to a cake

Choose your ribbon, then wrap it around the base of the cake and cut it so there is about a 1cm/½in overlap. Secure one end of the ribbon in place with a stainless steel pin, then fold the edge of the other end to neaten it. Wrap the ribbon tightly around the cake and secure the folded edge in place over the other end with some pearl-topped pins (available from specialist cake shops, haberdasheries/sewing notion stores or via websites). Depending on the width of ribbon, you'll need one, two or three pins.

16 Ribbon insertion

This is a simple but impressive way of decorating a cake covered with sugarpaste (gumpaste). Short lengths of ribbon are inserted at regular intervals into the surface of a cake covered with sugarpaste, giving the illusion of a piece of ribbon threaded through the icing. Different textures, widths and lengths of ribbon may be used to give this effect and, finished with bows or piping, make a stunning decoration.

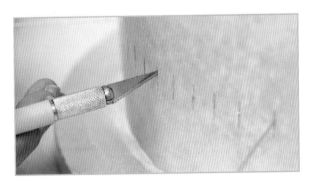

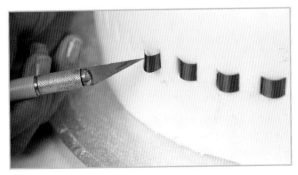

1 Take a strip of greaseproof (wax) paper the length of the cake diameter and mark vertical pairs of slots, each to the depth of your ribbon and about 1cm/½in apart leaving a short space between the pairs. Using pins, carefully fix the greaseproof paper to the sides of the cake. Then, using a small sharp knife (a scalpel is ideal), gently cut slots into the cake following the template marks.

2 Cut a strip of ribbon in the colour of your choice into sections of the desired length. Remove the paper and, using tweezers, a scalpel or a dedicated tool, insert one end of a ribbon piece into a slot. Bend the ribbon and push into the paired slot using the point of a knife or scalpel. Repeat around the cake.

Tiered cakes

If you are making a tiered cake, choose the sizes of tiers carefully, avoiding a combination that would look too heavy. A basic proportion for a three-tier cake is 30.5cm/12in, 23cm/9in and 15cm/6in. If in doubt, stack the empty cake tins on top of each other (base facing upwards) to give you a good idea of the finished proportions. Ideally, to give the cake balance, the depth of each tier should be the same. To ensure this, measure the depth of the uncooked mixture in the first cake tin. Take a note of this and ensure each subsequent cake mixture measures the same.

17 Assembling a royal iced cake using pillars

The solid pillars are placed directly on to the surface of the base cake, positioned accordingly and secured in place with a little royal icing before the next cake (which needs to be on a cake board) is placed on top.

Using pillars to separate tiers

Pillars are the traditional method of separating tiers of cakes. They are available, round or square, in a variety of heights, colours and patterns and some can be fitted with dowels inside, which will support the weight of very heavy cakes.

Using a template

For accurate assembling, cut out a paper template to the same size as the cake being supported above. Fold the template into four and place one pillar on the open corner of the template. Draw around the shape of the pillar and cut out. Open the template and place it on the centre of the base cake. Mark where the pillars need to go then remove the template. Repeat for the remaining tiers.

To use the template method for a round cake, fold the circular template of the supported cake into three, making a cone shape. Place one pillar on the edge of the broad end of the cone and draw around the shape. Cut out around the pillar shape. Open the template and place it on the centre of the base cake. Mark where the pillars need to be, then remove the template. Repeat for the remaining tiers.

Assembly on site

If you need to deliver your cake, always assemble it at home so you are happy with its appearance. Dismantle the cakes, leaving the dowels in position, and pack the cakes into boxes. Pack the pillars separately. Reassemble at your destination.

Tiers on a sugarpasted cake

If a sugarpasted (gumpasted) cake is to be supported by pillars, acrylic or wooden skewers – known as dowels – must be inserted into the cake since the icing will not support the weight of subsequent tiers. Pre-formed hollow cake pillars are then slipped over the dowels to conceal them and to support the cakes (which all need to be on cake boards). Arrange the hollow cake pillars on top of the cake until the position is right, then mark where the dowels should be. Use a paper template for positioning if required.

Insert a dowel into the centre of the positioned pillars and press vertically right through the icing into the cake until it is resting on the cake board. Continue inserting the dowels into the remaining pillars. Mark the dowels level with the top of each pillar. Carefully remove each pillar and dowel, and cut the dowels to the correct height following the marked lines. Replace the dowels and the pillars and position the cake. Repeat for the other tiers.

18 Stacking a sugarpasted cake

Smaller cakes covered with sugarpaste may be placed directly on top of each other to produce a soft, rounded effect, and are simply supported by their cake boards. It looks like the cakes are directly stacked one on top of the other, but actually the cake boards (which should be the same diameter as the cakes) are taking the weight – and where larger cakes are concerned, so are the dowels.

19 Dowelling a stacked cake

1 Using a pin, mark the diameter of the middle cake on top of the base (largest) cake. Measure a square within the diameter and push a dowel vertically into each corner until it reaches the bottom of the cake and stands on the base cake board.

2 Using a pencil, mark on each dowel where it emerges from the surface of the cake. Remove the dowel.

3 Using a craft knife, cut the dowels at the mark, all to the same length. Push back into the holes and spread royal icing over the centre of the base cake.

4 Put the next cake layer on top, then repeat the previous steps. Top with the last layer and decorate as desired.

Plastic or glass separators

Specialist cake shops or websites will sell plastic or glass cake separators – which are usually cubes or tubes. These are used instead of pillars and add a modern touch to a celebration cake. They can be filled with flowers, petals, crystals, pearls, coloured glass pebbles or foam beads, which can all be matched to the theme of the celebrations. Dowels will need to be added to support the corners of each separator.

Banana Cake

Cuts into 10 slices

Preparation time: 20 minutes
Cooking time: about 1 hour,
plus cooling

125g/4oz/1 stick unsalted butter,
   softened, plus extra to grease
125g/4oz/heaping ½ cup light
   muscovado (brown) sugar
2 large (US extra-large) eggs
50g/2oz smooth apple sauce
3 very ripe bananas, 375g/13oz
   peeled weight, mashed
1½ tsp mixed spice
150g/5oz/1 cup gluten-free plain
   (all-purpose) flour blend
1 tsp gluten-free baking powder
a pinch of salt

For the icing:
75g/3oz/¾ stick unsalted butter,
   softened
100g/3½oz/scant 1 cup icing
   (confectioners') sugar, sifted
50g/2oz/¼ cup light muscovado
   (brown) sugar
½ tbsp milk (optional)
Dried banana chips to decorate

PER SLICE: 363 cals; 18g fat (of which 11g
saturates); 50g carbohydrate; 0.4g salt

Gluten
free

1 Preheat the oven to 180°C (160°C fan oven)/350°F/Gas mark 4.
Grease the base and sides of a 900g/2lb loaf tin (pan) and line with
baking parchment (wax paper) **1**.

2 Using a hand-held electric whisk, beat the butter and muscovado
(brown) sugar in a large bowl until pale and creamy **2**. Lightly beat the
eggs, then gradually whisk them into the mixture, followed by the apple
sauce. Stir in the bananas.

3 Sift the spice, flour, baking powder and salt into the bowl, then use a
large metal spoon to fold in (the mixture may look a little curdled). Spoon
the mixture into the prepared tin.

4 Bake for 50 minutes to 1 hour until risen and a skewer inserted into
the centre comes out clean **3**. Leave to cool in the tin for 10 minutes,
then turn out on to a wire rack (leave the lining paper on) and leave to
cool completely. When the cake is cold, remove the lining paper and put
the cake on a serving plate.

5 To make the icing, whisk together the butter and both sugars until
smooth. If needed, add a little milk to loosen. Spread over the top of the
cooled cake. Decorate with banana chips. Serve in slices.

Simnel Cake

Cuts into 12 slices

Preparation time: 30 minutes
Cooking time: about 1 hour
25 minutes, plus cooling

225g/8oz/2 sticks butter, softened,
    plus extra to grease
225g/8oz/1½ cups self-raising
    (self-rising) flour
2 tsp ground mixed spice
400g/14oz/2⅔ cups mixed
    dried fruit
150g/5oz/heaping ¾ cup light
    muscovado (brown) sugar
50g/2oz golden (light corn) syrup
Finely grated zest of 2 lemons
4 medium (US large) eggs, lightly
    beaten

To decorate:

Icing (confectioners') sugar, to dust
500g/1lb 2oz almond paste
    (see page 33)
2 tbsp apricot jam (jelly)

Length of yellow ribbon

PER SLICE: 546 cals; 23g fat (of which 11g
saturates); 83g carbohydrate; 0.6g salt

Note

Simnel cake is the classic Easter
cake, its almond paste balls
representing the disciples – 11 or
12, depending on whether you
think Judas should be included.

1 Preheat the oven to 170°C (150°C fan oven)/325°F/Gas mark 3. Grease a 20.5cm/8in round cake tin (pan) with butter and line **1** with greaseproof (wax) paper or baking parchment.

2 In a large bowl, stir together the flour, mixed spice and dried fruit until combined. Put the butter, muscovado (brown) sugar, syrup and lemon zest into a separate large bowl and beat together using a hand-held electric whisk until pale and fluffy, about 3 minutes. Gradually beat in the eggs, whisking well after each addition. Add the flour mixture and fold everything together with a large metal spoon **2**.

3 Empty the mixture into the prepared tin and bake, covering with foil after 1 hour of cooking, for 1 hour 25 minutes, or until the cake is risen and springy to the touch **3**. A skewer inserted into the centre should come out clean, but don't be tempted to test too early or the cake may sink. Leave the cake to cool completely in the tin.

4 Take the cake out of the tin, peel off the paper and transfer to a serving plate. To decorate, dust the work surface with icing (confectioners') sugar and roll out two-thirds of the almond paste until large enough for a 20.5cm/8in circle (cut around the base of the cake tin). Heat the jam (jelly) with 1 tsp water in a small pan over a medium heat until runny. Brush the top of the cake with some jam, then lay the almond paste circle on top and gently press down to stick it to the cake. Using a small knife, score lines on top of the cake to make a diamond pattern. Crimp the edge of the almond paste using the thumb and forefinger of one hand, and the index finger of the other.

5 Roll the remaining almond paste into 11 equal-sized balls. Brush the underside of each with a little jam or water and stick to the top of the cake. If you like, use a blowtorch to lightly brown the almond paste. To finish, secure a yellow ribbon **15** around the side of the cake.

Graduation Cake

Cuts into about 20 slices

Preparation time: 1½ hours
Cooking time: about 40 minutes,
plus cooling, setting and drying

Unsalted butter to grease
2 × base Carrot Cake mixture
    (see page 27)
About 150g/5oz white sugarpaste
    (gumpaste), plus extra to cover
    the board
Icing (confectioners') sugar, sifted,
    to dust
500g/1lb 2oz plain (semi-sweet)
    chocolate cocoform (modelling
    chocolate)
Thick glacé icing to pipe
    (see page 32)

For the frosting:
50g/2oz/½ stick butter, preferably
    unsalted, at room temperature
225g/8oz pack cream cheese
25g/1oz/2 tsp golden icing
    (confectioners') sugar
½ tsp vanilla extract

Large square cake board
Sheet of rice paper
Ribbon (optional)

PER SLICE: 613 cals; 38g fat (of which 13g
saturates); 67g carbohydrate; 0.6g salt

1 Preheat the oven to 180°C (160°C fan oven)/350°F/Gas mark 4. Grease and line **1** two 20.5cm/8in square roasting tins (pans) (they don't need to be very deep). Make up the carrot cake mixture and divide between the prepared tins. Bake for 40 minutes or until a skewer inserted into the centre comes out clean **3**. Leave to cool in the tins for 10 minutes, then transfer to a wire rack to cool completely.

2 Meanwhile, cover the cake board in white sugarpaste (gum paste) **12** and leave to harden. To make the frosting, beat the butter and cream cheese together in a bowl until light and fluffy. Sift in the icing (confectioners') sugar, add the vanilla extract and beat well until smooth.

3 Trim each cake into a book-shaped rectangle and cut both rectangles in half horizontally **4**. Use some of the frosting to sandwich the rectangles back together, then lightly cover each with more frosting. Leave to set for 30 minutes.

4 Lightly dust a work surface with icing sugar and roll out half of the white sugarpaste (gumpaste) to about a 5mm/¼in thickness. Cut into a strip slightly wider than the depth of the cake, and long enough to wrap around two of the short sides and one long side of the cake. Use a knife to mark the strip into what looks like pages. Wrap the strip around the cake **11** (one long side should be left free). Repeat the process with the other cake.

5 Roll out about 250g/9oz cocoform (modelling chocolate) until it is about 5mm/¼in thick. Cut out a wide strip long enough to cover the top, one side and back of one cake. Position the strip on to the cake, press down lightly and trim any excess. Roll out the remaining cocoform and repeat to cover the other cake. Leave to dry.

6 When the cakes have hardened, stack on the iced cake board **18**. Use a little thick glacé icing to pipe **23** subjects on the spines of the books, and a message on the board, if you like. Roll up some rice paper and tie with the ribbon to make a scroll. Fix on to the books with a little glacé icing. Leave the cake to dry.

Cocoform is available from specialist cake shops or via websites.

Fresh Flower Wedding Cake

Cuts into 150 small slices

To decorate: 45 minutes

1 × 15cm/6in, 1 × 20.5cm/8in
   and 1 × 25.5cm/10in round
   Rich Fruit Cake (see page
   24), almond-pasted **9** and
   sugarpasted (gumpasted) **11**
Extra sugarpaste (optional)

Dowels
1 × 15cm/6in, 1 × 20.5cm/8in
   and 1 × 25.5cm/10in round
   cake board
12.5cm/5in and 7.5cm/3in
   polystyrene (styrofoam)
   dummies
Ribbon (optional)
Fresh flowers
Florists' (covered) wire (optional)
Toothpick or skewer (optional)
Flower pick (optional)

PER SLICE: 277 cals; 11g fat (of which 6g
saturates); 38g carbohydrate; 0.2g salt

1   Measure and dowel **19** your base-layer sugarpasted (gumpasted) cake (which should be on a cake board) to the same dimensions as the polystyrene (styrofoam) dummy. The dummy needs to be a good few inches smaller than the cake on which it is sitting but the size varies depending on the depth of the flower, the size of the cake and the desired end result. As a general guide the dummy should be 7.5cm/3in smaller than the tier it is supporting.

2   Sit the dummy centrally on the base layer of cake and top with the next layer of the sugarpasted cake (which also needs to be on a cake board) **18**. Repeat the process, if necessary, with another dummy and a final top tier. Cover the edges of the cake boards with ribbon if they are showing. Trim the cakes with other ribbons **15**, as you like. Disassemble the cake and store until needed.

3   On the day of the celebration prepare your fresh flowers. Trim the stems of the flowers (if necessary) to about 5cm/2in and split any larger blooms (such as hydrangeas) into smaller, more regular sections. Wrap the stems with florists' (covered) wire to strengthen them if necessary – roses and other hardier flowers are stiff enough, whereas gerberas will need strengthening.

4   Stack the cakes with the dummies in between the layers. Now insert the flowers into the dummies (you might need to poke a hole into the dummy with a toothpick or skewer to help the flower insertion), filling until you can no longer see any polystyrene.

5   If you want to top your cake with more fresh flowers, either use a flower pick or press a lump of soft sugarpaste on to the top tier, then insert flowers into the sugarpaste. To prevent the flowers from wilting, make sure the cake is kept out of direct sunlight.

Choosing flowers
When using fresh flowers that will be in close contact with the cake, always buy non-toxic flowers that have not been treated with chemicals. Roses, gerbera and hydrangeas work particularly well and give a good visual result.

Using polystyrene dummies

If you wish to display a lot of fresh flowers on a wedding cake without using numerous flower picks (see below), then polystyrene (styrofoam) dummies are the answer. These can be stuffed with fresh flowers, which will give the effect of floating floral layers between sugarpasted cakes.

Using flower picks

Avoid sticking the stems of the flowers straight into the sugarpasted cake, as you run the risk of introducing germs. Instead, use food-safe flower picks that can be inserted into your cake and safely hold flowers in position. Flower picks are available in a range of sizes and shapes from specialist cake shops or websites and can hold anything from a single stem to a larger spray.

Classic Christmas Cake

Cuts into 24 slices

Preparation time: 30 minutes, plus soaking
Cooking time: about 4 hours, plus cooling

500g/1lb 2oz/2½ cups sultanas (golden raisins)
400g/14oz/2⅔ cups raisins
150g/5oz/1 cup each Agen prunes and dried figs, roughly chopped
200g/7oz/1⅓ cups dried apricots, roughly chopped
zest and juice of 2 oranges
200ml/7fl oz hazelnut liqueur, such as Frangelico hazelnut liqueur, plus extra to drizzle
250g/9oz/2¼ sticks unsalted butter, softened, plus extra to grease
150g/5oz/heaping ¾ cup each dark muscovado (brown) and light brown soft sugar
200g/7oz/1⅓ cups plain (all-purpose) flour, sifted
1 tsp ground cinnamon
1 tsp mixed spice
¼ tsp ground cloves
¼ tsp freshly grated nutmeg
Pinch of salt
4 large (US extra large) eggs, beaten
100g/3½oz/½ cup toasted, blanched hazelnuts, roughly chopped
40g (1½oz) toasted pine nuts
1 tbsp brandy (optional)

For the icing:

Preparation time: 30 minutes, plus drying
Cooking time: 3–4 minutes, plus cooling

4 tbsp apricot jam (jelly)
Icing (confectioners') sugar, sifted, to dust
450g/1lb packet ready-to-roll almond paste
Vegetable oil to grease

150g/5oz glacier mint sweets (candies)
500g/1lb 2oz packet royal icing sugar

75 × 2cm/30 × ¼in silver ribbon
Silver candles

PER SERVING (INCLUDING CAKE):
569 cals; 17g fat (of which 6g saturates); 100g carbohydrate; 0.2g salt

1 Put the fruit into a non-metallic bowl and stir in the orange zest and juice and the hazelnut liqueur. Cover and leave to soak overnight or, preferably, up to three days.

2 Preheat the oven to 140°C (120°C fan oven)/275°F/ Gas mark 1. Grease a 23cm/9in cake tin (pan) and double-line **1** with greaseproof (wax) paper, making sure the paper comes at least 5cm/2in above the top of the tin. Grease the paper lightly. Then wrap a double layer of greaseproof paper around the outside of the tin, securing with string to stop the cake burning.

3 Using a hand-held electric mixer, beat together the butter and sugars in a large bowl until light and fluffy – this should take about 5 minutes **2**.

4 In a separate bowl, sift together the flour, spices and salt. Beat 2 tbsp of the flour mixture into the butter and sugar, then gradually add the eggs, making sure the mixture doesn't curdle. If it looks as if it might be about to, add a little more flour.

5 Using a large metal spoon, fold the remaining flour into the mixture, followed by the soaked fruit and the nuts. Tip into the prepared tin and level the surface. Using the end of the spoon, make a hole in the centre of the mix, going right down to the base of the tin – this will stop the top of the cake rising into a dome shape as it cooks. Bake for 4 hours or until a skewer inserted into the centre comes out clean **3**. Cover with foil if it is browning too quickly. Leave to cool in the tin for 10 minutes, then turn out on to a wire rack, keeping the greaseproof paper wrapped around the outside of the cake, and leave to cool completely.

6 To store, leave the cold cake in its greaseproof paper. Wrap a few layers of cling film (plastic wrap) around it, then cover with foil. Store in a cool place in an airtight container. After two weeks, unwrap the cake, prick all over and pour over 1 tbsp of hazelnut liqueur, or brandy if you prefer. Rewrap and store as before. Ice up to three days before serving (see right).

Icing the cake

1 Gently heat the jam (jelly) in a pan with 1 tbsp water until softened, then press through a sieve into a bowl to make a smooth glaze. Put the cake on a board and brush over the top and sides with the glaze.

2 Dust a rolling pin and the work surface with a little icing (confectioners') sugar and roll out the almond paste to a round about 15cm/6in larger than the cake. Position over the cake and ease to fit around the sides, pressing out any creases **8**. Trim off the excess around the base. Leave to dry for 24 hours.

3 Preheat the oven to 180°C (160°C fan oven)/350°F/ Gas mark 4. Line a baking sheet with foil and brush lightly with oil. Unwrap the mints and put pairs of sweets (candies) on the baking sheet about 1cm/½in apart, leaving 5cm/2in of space between each pair, to allow room for them to spread as they melt. Cook for 3–4 minutes until the sweets have melted and are just starting to bubble around the edges. Leave to cool on the foil for 3–4 minutes until firm enough to be lifted off. Use kitchen scissors to snip the pieces into large slivers and shards.

4 Wrap the ribbon all around the edge of the cake **15**. Put the icing sugar in a bowl and make up according to the pack instructions. Using a small palette knife, spread the icing over the top of the cake **10**, flicking it into small peaks as you go. Then tease the edges of the icing down the sides of the cake to form icicles.

5 While the icing is still soft, push the mint shards into the top of the cake and insert the silver candles. Leave the cake to dry. Light the candles and serve.

Piping

Piping is one of the most traditional skills, used to decorate all types of cakes. It takes some practice to master, but the skill will come in useful frequently when decorating cakes. Just by varying the pressure, angle and nozzle (tip) shape and size you can produce many different designs with quite simple equipment.

Piping decoration

The only equipment you need is a piping (decorating) bag and a good set of nozzles (tips). Make up a batch of royal icing and start practising by piping on boards, around cake tins (pans) and on to plates – that way you can reuse the icing time and again until you are competent. Try simple piping first with basic nozzles, then as your skill and consistency improve, proceed to a larger selection of nozzles and techniques.

20 Making a paper icing bag

Reusable and disposable icing bags are widely available, but it's just as easy to make your own from greaseproof (wax) paper. Often delicate piping work is easiest achieved with a homemade icing bag, which can be snipped to a fine tip or used in conjunction with a piping nozzle (tip). Once you've mastered the technique, make a batch of bags so that you have some ready and waiting. The bag can simply be disposed of once you have finished with it – just remember to rescue any piping nozzles first.

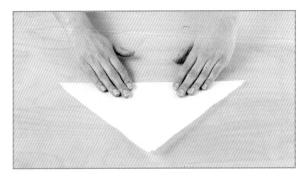

1   Cut out a rectangle of greaseproof (wax) paper measuring about 25.5 × 20.5cm / 10 × 8in – for smaller bags, cut a proportionally smaller rectangle. Fold in half diagonally, then cut along the crease. Use one of the triangles to continue.

2   Put the paper on the work surface with the apex of the triangle nearest to you. Bring the top left-hand point round to line up with the bottom point. Hold in place with your thumb and index finger.

3   Bring the right-hand point over and round the back, meeting at the bottom point. Pull together slightly to tighten the point. Fold over the points of the paper nearest to you to secure the bag.

4   To use, fill with icing and fold the paper over to seal. Snip the point off the bag (either straight across or at a slant), or fit with a metal nozzle (tip) before filling for more intricate designs.

Piping techniques

21 Filling a piping bag

1 If using a nozzle (tip), snip off the tip of the piping (decorating) bag and drop in a nozzle. If not using a nozzle, then leave the tip intact. If using a plastic piping bag, fold the top over to make a collar.

2 Hold the piping bag in your hand or stand it in a bowl or jug to support it. Fill half to two-thirds with icing. If using plastic, unfold the collar and twist to tighten to the level of the icing. Snip the tip if needed (either straight across or at a slant) and squeeze the bag gently to remove air bubbles and start the icing flowing. If using paper, fold over the open end until you hit the icing, then snip the tip if needed and squeeze the bag gently to remove air bubbles and start the icing flowing.

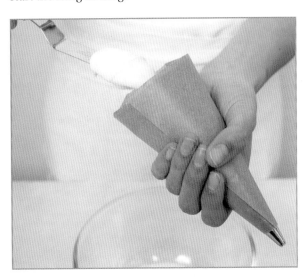

3 Never over-fill a piping bag, as it will become difficult to handle and as you squeeze, the icing will ooze out of the top. A good rule to remember is the smaller the piping nozzle, the smaller the piping bag and the less icing you require.

It is essential to have the buttercream, royal icing or whipped cream at the correct consistency – when a wooden spoon is drawn out it should form a fine sharp point. If the icing is too stiff, it will be difficult to pipe; if too soft the icing will run too freely, be difficult to control and lose definition. The larger the nozzle (tip), the stiffer the icing needs to be; for a fine writing nozzle, the consistency needs to be looser.

Piping tips

- Pipe small amounts of cream at a time – over-handling in the piping (decorating) bag can cause it to curdle. Use larger nozzles (tips) to pipe cream.
- Keep your work area clean to avoid crumbs, dirt or blemishes appearing on your finished cake.
- Plan your pattern and prick out a design with a pin to give you a template **24** to follow when piping.
- Pipe intricate designs onto silicone paper to dry, then fix onto the cake with a dab of royal icing.
- Cover a bowl of icing with damp kitchen paper (paper towels), cling film (plastic wrap) or a tea towel to prevent it drying out.
- Practise first – a board, cake tin (pan) or upturned plate make good surfaces.

22 Piping designs

❶ Lines

Fit a piping (decorating) bag with a plain or star nozzle (tip) – the smaller the hole, the finer the lines. Hold the piping bag at a 45-degree angle and 5mm/¼in above the surface, then pipe towards you, securing the beginning of the line to the surface with a little pressure. Raise the bag slightly as the icing flows on to the surface in a straight or curved line. Press the piping bag to the surface lightly to secure the line, then pull away sharply to finish.

❷ Beads

The size of bead depends on the nozzle (tip) used and the pressure applied to the piping (decorating) bag. Start with icing of slightly softer consistency so there are no sharp points on the ends of the beads. Hold the nozzle upright just above the surface, then squeeze out some icing onto the surface to make a bead (keeping the nozzle still). Pull up sharply to break the icing. Make another bead next to the first one to make a chain. Smooth off the beads with a damp finger if necessary.

❸ Rosettes/roses

Fit a piping (decorating) bag with a star nozzle (tip). Hold the piping bag straight above the surface, with the nozzle just touching the surface. Press out some icing to the size of the rosette you want, lifting the bag slightly to give the rosette space. Stop pressing, then pull up sharply to break the icing. Repeat next to the first rosette to make a border.

❹ Filigree

Fit a piping (decorating) bag with a writing nozzle (tip). Hold the piping bag with the nozzle like a pen, between thumb and index finger. Pipe a thread of icing onto the cake in the desired pattern. Keep the flow constant and work in all directions without breaking the thread for as long as possible. Re-join the icing where the break finished to keep the design constant.

❺ Shell

Fit a piping (decorating) bag with a star nozzle (tip). Hold the piping bag at a 45-degree angle and 5mm/¼in above the surface. Pipe a small blob of icing and secure to the surface with a little pressure, then bring the bag slowly up, over the blob a little, then towards you and down again – almost like a rocking movement. Pull away sharply to finish off the shell. Pipe the next shell over the end of the previous one to make an edging.

❻ Rope/barrel

Fit a piping (decorating) bag with a star nozzle (tip). To pipe a rope, hold the piping bag at a 45-degree angle and 5mm/¼in above the surface. Pipe a line in a continuous spiral motion. To make a barrel shape, gradually increase the pressure on the bag as you reach the middle of the line and then decrease the pressure towards the end.

❼ Lattice/trellis

Fit a piping (decorating) bag with a fine, plain nozzle (tip). Pipe parallel lines about 5mm/¼in apart, keeping them as even as possible. Over-pipe parallel lines (keeping the spacing the same) at 90-degrees to the initial lines. A third layer of piping can be piped diagonally to the initial layers for an intricate finish.

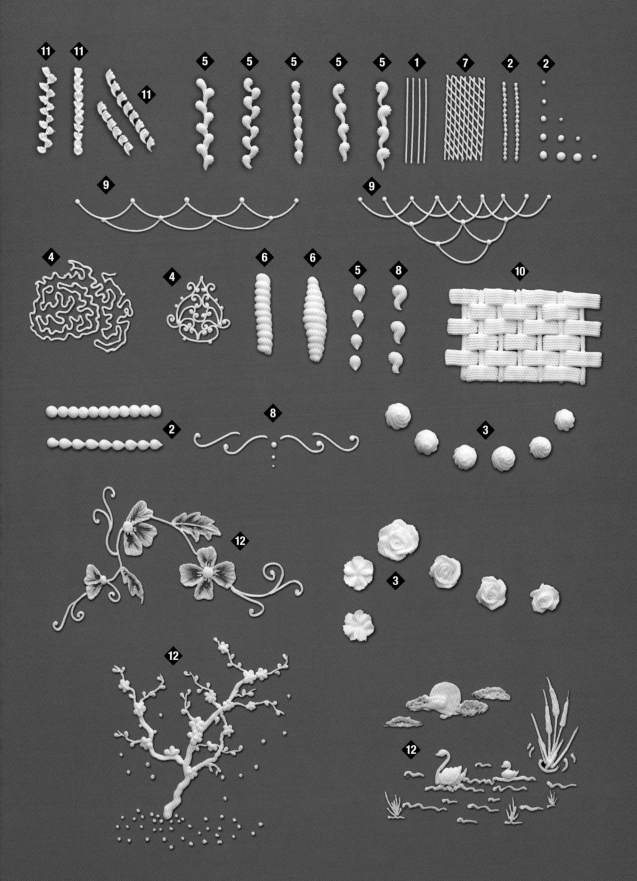

❽ Scroll

Fit a piping (decorating) bag with a star nozzle (tip). Hold the piping bag at a 45-degree angle and 5mm/¼in above the surface. Pipe the shape of a question mark (without the dot), then pull off sharply to break the icing. Repeat with another swirl (alternating directions, if you like).

❾ Dropped-thread loop work

Fit a piping (decorating) bag with a fine, plain nozzle (tip). Pipe a thread of icing, securing the end to the side of the cake. Continue to pipe the icing just away from the side of the cake so the thread forms a loop. Stop squeezing the piping bag when the loop is almost long enough, then press the thread of icing gently onto the side of the cake to secure and break off the icing. Repeat until the loops go right round the cake. It is possible to over-pipe each loop in the same or different colour icing – start your over-piped loop halfway across the first.

❿ Basket weave

Pipe a plain vertical line from the top of the cake to the bottom. Fit another piping (decorating) bag with a ribbon nozzle (tip) – this will produce a half plain, half fluted pipe. The finer the nozzle, the more intricate the finished weave will look. Starting at the top of the cake, pipe 2cm/¾in lines of icing horizontally across the vertical line at 1cm/½in intervals. Now pipe another plain vertical line on the right-hand edge of the horizontal lines, then pipe 2cm/¾in horizontal lines, starting between the first horizontal lines and going over the second vertical line. Repeat the process to give a basket weave.

⓫ Leaves/leaf ropes

Fit a piping (decorating) bag with a leaf nozzle (tip). Hold the bag so the point of the nozzle faces forward. Squeeze the bag hard to pipe the base of the leaf, then release so the leaf trails off to a point. To make a leaf rope, pipe one leaf then start another below it and continue so they are connected like a rope. Or pipe leaves on alternate sides.

⓬ Lace work

Often used on wedding cakes, lace piping is delicate work. Designs can be piped directly onto cakes or small sections can be piped onto non-stick paper and left to dry before being fixed to the cake. Try to have lots of lines touching in the design to make the lace work stronger and prevent breakages.

1 Draw your design on a piece of paper. Repeat it several times, so once you start piping you can continue. Put the design on a flat surface and cover with a piece of run-on film, waxed paper or baking parchment. Secure the edges with tape or icing.

2 Use run-out decoration consistency icing (see page 34) so the designs dry hard. Fit a small piping (decorating) bag with a no. 0 plain nozzle (tip), then quarter-fill the bag with icing and fold down the top.

3 With the nozzle held very closely to the surface, and under even pressure, pipe your design. Large pieces may be over-piped to give them double strength.

4 Pipe more pieces than required to allow for breakages. Leave the pieces to dry, then run a fine palette knife (metal spatula) under them to release.

5 Attach the lace pieces to the cake with beads of royal icing. If the lace pieces need to be stored or transported, leave them on the run-on film or paper and pack carefully, interleaved with tissue paper, into cardboard boxes.

23 To pipe writing

Use fine, plain nozzles (tips) and practise before attempting writing on a cake. Work out how much space the letters take, and choose a style of handwriting. If you are unsure about piping freehand, trace the word(s) onto greaseproof (wax) paper and, using a scribing needle or pin, mark along the letters in tiny dots – pipe the letters by connecting the dots. Alternatively, write your message onto a dried sugar- or flowerpaste (gumpaste) plaque and attach to the cake with a little water or royal icing.

Piping directly on to a cake

Use royal icing for intricate and delicate cake decorating work, as it sets hard and lasts for months. Lines and borders are best piped directly on to the cake, while more intricate shapes can be piped on to silicone paper, left to dry then, fixed on to the cake with a dab of royal icing. Whole sheets of decorations can be piped on to silicone paper and stored like this in an airtight container for several weeks.

24 Making and using template

To avoid mistakes and to ensure your design is symmetrical, it is best to make a template first.

1 Draw a pattern on greaseproof (wax) paper cut to the same size as the top or sides of the cake. For a tiered wedding cake you will need a proportionally sized template for each cake (and only the edges of most tiers will be visible). To make a scalloped edge to a circle template, fold your template in half several times and use a compass (or the edge of a jar) to mark the curved edge, and then cut out this curve.

2 Attach the template to the surface or sides of your cake with a pin.

3 Prick the surface with another pin, following the lines of your design.

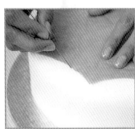

4 Alternatively, you can prick the outline of the design using a scribing needle. Remove the paper and pipe over the pin marks.

25 Filling piped shapes

For these, outlines are piped with royal icing on to cakes, biscuits or templates and flooding icing is used to fill shapes. Any shape or form can be made by tracing over a design or pattern, but they are fragile so it is wise to start with a small solid shape and progress from there. To make flooding icing, thin down royal icing with a drop at a time of tepid water. Stir well after each addition until the desired consistency is reached (see piping consistency on page 34). Don't beat, just stir or you will add air bubbles to the design. When using different colours on one design, allow each one to dry before adding the next.

1   Fit a piping (decorating) bag with a fine, plain nozzle (tip). Place a drawing of your chosen design under a piece of run-out film (or waxed paper). Using royal icing thick enough for piping writing, pipe the outline of the design directly onto the run-out or waxed paper, following the drawing below. Make sure the outline of each section of the design is closed, so the flooding icing doesn't leak when applied.

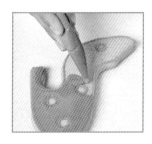

2   Fill another piping bag with the flooding icing (a nozzle isn't necessary), snip off the end and fill in the piped shapes, ensuring that the icing floods up to the edge of the outline. Fill so the icing looks rounded, not flat, as it will shrink on drying. If needed, use a fine paintbrush to coax icing into small areas. Burst any air bubbles with a pin.

3   Leave to dry completely (at least 24 hours). Pipe any details on to the run-outs at this stage and allow to dry again.

4   Using a fine palette knife (metal spatula), release the design from the film or paper and attach to the cake with a few beads of royal icing; alternatively, store on the film or paper, interleaved with tissue paper, in a cardboard box for a few months.

26 Piping flowers and leaves

With the use of a petal nozzle and royal icing, many simple flower shapes can be piped. The nozzles come in a range of sizes, each suited to piping different size flowers. They are also available for left or right-handers. Colour the icing to your desired hue.

Basic flower

1   Fit a piping (decorating) bag with a petal nozzle (tip). Half-fill the bag 21 with 'sharp peak' consistency (see page 34) royal icing. Fold down the open end of the bag to seal. If you have one, use an icing nail (like a mini turntable) with a small square of parchment paper on it, otherwise just use the paper.

2   Start by piping a petal – keep an even pressure and pipe a closed horseshoe shape (many modern icing (flower) nails will have dimensions of petals drawn on to them to help guide you). Slowly rotate the spinner (or manually rotate the paper if you don't have an icing nail) as you pipe the second petal.

3   By the time you pipe the third petal, two-thirds of the flower should be piped. If not, the petals are too fat or too thin. Keep rotating to pipe the remaining two petals. Pipe a contrasting bead of icing in the centre and leave to dry completely.

4   Remove the flower and attach to your cake with a bead of royal icing. Blush the blossoms with some colour or lustre dust, if you like.

Leaves

1   Make a small greaseproof (wax) paper piping bag **20**, fill with your desired leaf colour icing and cut the end of the piping bag into an inverted 'v'.

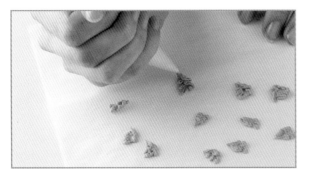

2   Put the tip of the piping bag directly on to the surface of the cake, or on to some waxed paper. Press out icing to form a leaf shape. Repeat to make as many leaves as you want (or attach to make a border). Leave to dry on waxed paper. Remove and attach to your cake with a bead of royal icing.

27 Feather icing

Feathering is an easy technique that will create elegant results on cakes or cupcakes. It works best using glacé icing. To feather ice 12 small cakes, you will need 225g/8oz glacé icing (see page 32).

1   The top of the cupcakes needs to be fairly flat for feathering to work. If they have risen, trim away the peak and dust away any crumbs with your fingers. Put the cakes on a flat surface.

2   Divide the icing into two. Now choose colours, but they need to contrast well for the feathering to stand out. Most classic is to leave the base colour white and dye the other bowl of icing with cocoa powder, or use a food colouring paste.

3   Cover six cakes with white icing and six with coloured icing, spooning on just enough to cover. Spread the icing to the edge of each cake with the help of a small palette knife (metal spatula) or teaspoon.

4   Spoon the remaining icings into two separate small piping bags (decorating bags) (without nozzles/tips). Snip off the tips (finely) and, working quickly, pipe parallel lines 5mm/¼in apart, or concentric circles, on top of the cakes in a contrasting colour.

5   Draw a cocktail stick or fine pointed knife through the piped icing in one direction and then in the opposite direction to create the feather pattern. Work quickly or the icing will form a skin and set before the pattern has been formed. Leave to set.

Ballet Cake

Cuts into about 16 slices
(or more for little mouths!)

Preparation time: 1½ hours
Cooking time: about 1½ hours,
plus cooling, setting and drying

Unsalted butter to grease
1 × 18cm/7in round cake tin (pan)
 quantity Madeira Cake mixture
 (see page 29)
100–125g/3½–4oz white
 sugarpaste (gumpaste)
Pink food colouring paste
Lustre dust (optional)
Edible glue (optional)
500g/1lb 2oz buttercream
 (see page 32)
400g/14oz vanilla frosting
 (see page 35)
Pink sugar crystals (optional)

4 short lengths of pale pink
 satin ribbon
1 cake stand
Piping (decorating) bag and
 petal leaf nozzle (tip)

PER SLICE: 463 cals; 20g fat (of which 11g
saturates); 73g carbohydrate; 0.4g salt

1 Preheat the oven to 170°C (150°C fan oven)/325°F/Gas mark 3. Grease and line **1** a deep 18cm/7in round cake tin (pan). Fill the tin with the Madeira cake mixture and bake for 1¼–1½ hours until the cake is golden on top and a skewer inserted into the centre comes out clean **3**. Leave to cool for 10 minutes in the tin, then cool completely on a wire rack.
2 While the cake is cooling, tint the sugarpaste (gumpaste) to light pink (ballet slipper colour). Divide the sugarpaste in half and roll one half into a sausage shape. Using your fingers, press into the top of the shape to form a slipper, leaving the cap of the shoe in place. Make the slipper narrower in the middle and as delicate as possible. Brush the slipper with lustre dust and, with the help of a small knife, insert two short lengths of ribbon in place (alternatively, stick the ribbon to the outside of the shoes with edible glue). Put onto a sheet of greaseproof (wax) paper or baking parchment. Repeat with the other slipper and leave to dry for at least 3 hours (or make the day before and allow to dry overnight).
3 Slice the cooled cake into three even layers **4**. Dye the buttercream to a darker shade of pink. Sandwich the cake layers back together using some of the buttercream. Put the cake on a turntable. Lightly spread buttercream on the sides **5**, then cover the top generously and neatly. Leave to set for 30 minutes, then transfer to a cake stand.
4 Dye 350g/12oz vanilla frosting pale pink. Fit a piping (decorating) bag with a petal leaf nozzle (tip) and fill with the frosting **21**. Holding the bag nearly vertical so that the tip (narrow end facing outwards) is by the base of the cake, create a ruffle **22** by squeezing the bag while making a 2.5cm/1in wide quick back and forth motion, at the same time moving the nozzle up the side of the cake. Finish the ruffle at the top edge of the cake, pulling off as neatly as possible. Repeat ruffling all around the cake.
5 Sprinkle pink sugar crystals, if using, over the top of the cake. Dye the remaining frosting with a hint of pink and pipe a border **22** around the top edge of the cake, then position the slippers and ribbons. Leave to dry.

Making ruffles
Inspired by the many layers of a ballerina tutu, this cake is sure to delight any young girl. You will need a petal nozzle (shaped like a narrow teardrop) to create these dramatic ruffles.

Secret Garden Cupcakes

Makes 12

Preparation time: 45 minutes
Cooking time: 40 minutes,
plus cooling

200g/7oz/1⅓ cups fresh
    strawberries, hulled and halved
200g/7oz/¾ cup caster sugar
150g/5oz/1¼ sticks unsalted
    butter, softened
3 medium (US large) eggs
200g/7oz/1⅓ cups self-raising
    (self-rising) flour, sifted
½ tsp bicarbonate of soda
    (baking soda)
50ml/2fl oz buttermilk

For the icing:
125g/4oz/1 stick unsalted butter,
    softened
250g/9oz/2 cups icing
    (confectioners') sugar, sifted
Green food colouring
Ladybird (ladybug), bumble bee
    and butterfly sugar decorations
    (optional)

Piping (decorating) bag and
    star nozzle (tip)

PER CUPCAKE: 398 cals; 20g fat (of which
13g saturates); 53g carbohydrate; 0.5g salt

1   Preheat the oven to 190°C (170°C fan oven)/375°F/Gas mark 5. Line a 12-hole muffin tin (pan) with paper muffin cases (liners).

2   Put the strawberries and 50g/2oz/¼ cup of caster sugar into a heatproof bowl and cover with cling film (plastic wrap). Put over a pan of barely simmering water and cook gently for 30 minutes.

3   Meanwhile, using a hand-held electric whisk, whisk the butter and remaining caster sugar in a bowl **2**, or beat with a wooden spoon, until pale and creamy. Gradually whisk in the eggs until just combined. Using a metal spoon, fold in the flour, bicarbonate of soda (baking soda) and buttermilk until combined. Divide the mixture equally among all the paper cases.

4   Bake for 20 minutes or until golden and risen. Leave to cool in the tin for 5 minutes. Meanwhile, pass the strawberries and juice through a sieve into a shallow bowl. Discard the strawberries.

5   Using a cocktail stick, prick the top of the cakes all over. Dip the top of each cake into the strawberry syrup, then transfer to a wire rack to cool completely.

6   For the topping, put the butter into a bowl and whisk until fluffy. Gradually whisk in half the icing (confectioners') sugar, then add 1 tbsp boiling water, a little green food colouring and the remaining icing sugar and whisk until light and fluffy.

7   Insert a star nozzle (tip) into a piping (decorating) bag, then fill the bag **21** with the buttercream and pipe in a zigzag pattern on top of each cake **22**. Decorate with the sugar ladybirds (ladybugs), butterflies and bumble bees, if you like.

Firework Cupcakes

Makes 12

Preparation time: 30 minutes
Cooking time: 20 minutes, plus cooling and setting

125g/4oz/1 scant cup self-raising (self-rising) flour
1 tsp baking powder
125g/4oz/scant ½ cup caster sugar
125g/4oz/1 stick butter or soft margarine
2 large (US extra-large) eggs
Grated zest of 2 large unwaxed lemons, plus extra shreds, to decorate (optional)
1 tbsp freshly squeezed lemon juice

For the icing and decoration:
1 × quantity glacé icing (see page 32)
Gel food colourings
2 tbsp royal icing (see page 33)
Edible glitter (optional)
Dragees (multicoloured if possible)

3–4 piping bags (decorating bags) and fine nozzles (tips)

PER CUPCAKE: 254 cals; 10g fat (of which 2g

saturates); 42g carbohydrate; 0.4g salt

1   Preheat the oven to 190°C (170°C fan oven)/375°F/Gas mark 5. Line a 12-hole muffin tin (pan) with paper muffin cases (liners).

2   Sift the flour, baking powder and sugar into a large bowl, food processor or mixer. Add the butter/margarine, eggs, lemon zest and juice and beat until light and fluffy **2**.

3   Spoon the mixture into the cases and bake for about 20 minutes until firm to the touch and golden. Transfer to a wire rack to cool completely.

4   For the icing, make up the glacé icing and add deep navy blue to imitate the night sky. Add the icing to each cake **13** and allow the icing to dry completely.

5   Separate the royal icing into as many bowls as you want colours, and tint them accordingly with the food colouring. Using piping bags (decorating bags) with fine nozzles (tips), pipe on **22** whatever firework you like such as Catherine wheels, rockets and shooting stars.

6   Sprinkle a tiny bit of edible glitter over them if you want, and add the dragees, which may need a tiny dab of royal icing underneath them to hold them in place.

Dinosaur Cake

Cuts into about 30 slices

Preparation time: 1½ hours
Cooking time: about 2 hours, plus cooling, setting and drying

Butter to grease
3 × 175g/6oz butter quantity
    Madeira Cake mixtures
    (see page 29)
1.5kg/3¼lb buttercream
    (see page 32)
Yellow, blue, black, purple, red
    and brown (optional) food
    colouring pastes
White almond paste (see page 33)
    to model

30.5cm/12in round cake board
Piping (decorating) bag
1 × 5mm/¼in piping nozzle (tip)

PER SLICE: 569 cals; 30g fat (of which 18g
saturates); 74g carbohydrate; 0.7g salt

1 Preheat the oven to 170°C (150°C fan oven)/325°F/ Gas mark 3. Grease a 23cm/9in round cake tin (pan) and line **1** with greaseproof (wax) paper, then grease the paper lightly again. Do the same with a roasting tin, roughly 15 × 20.5cm/6 × 8in. Divide the Madeira cake mixture between the prepared tins, making sure that each tin is about half full. Bake for 1¾–2 hours or until the cakes are golden and a skewer inserted into the centre comes out clean **3**. Leave the cakes to cool for 15 minutes in the tin, then transfer to a wire rack to cool completely.

2 When the cakes are completely cool, cut the round cake in half to make two semi-circles **4**. Stand the two semi-circles side-by-side on their cut sides on the side of the cake board. This will form the body of the dinosaur.

3 Cut a 7.5cm/3in wide strip off the entire length of one of the short edges of the rectangular cake. Cut this in half horizontally down the middle to make two smaller cakes **4**. Stack these cakes on top of one another to make the rough head, then carve with a knife to give the head a more realistic shape. Position the head a little way away from the body on the side of the board and bridge the body and the head with extra cake to make the neck. Use more of the rectangular cake to cut out the back leg shape and the wide part of the tail. Finally, use a knife to carve the back of the dinosaur down a little so that it meets the tail and neck well. Use some of these rounded trimmings to make the narrower end of the tail.

4 Once you are happy with the positioning of the carved dinosaur on the board, use some of the buttercream to sandwich the cake into position. If any gaps appear, then use trimmings to fill them up. Brush away any crumbs from the cake board.

5 Divide the remaining buttercream equally among three bowls. Using yellow and blue food colourings, colour the buttercream in two of the bowls green – making one a brighter green and one a darker,

duller green. Add a touch of black (optional) to make both greens more reptilian. Now remove 2 tbsp buttercream from the remaining white buttercream bowl. Colour what is left in the bowl bright purple, then dull it down with a little black. Colour the reserved 2 tbsp buttercream red, cover and set aside.

6 Fit a 5mm/¼in nozzle (tip) into a piping (decorating) bag. Two-thirds fill the piping bag **21** by dolloping in spoonfuls of alternating greens and purple (the marble effect will create a more realistic dinosaur skin). Or, if you like, pipe onto the cake in alternate colours, creating a striped effect.

7 Starting at the back of the dinosaur, pipe on the buttercream. You can either do neat beads **22**, or join the beads together by not pulling the piping bag off completely before starting on the next bead. Cover the whole dinosaur in this way (filling the bag as before when needed). Leave to set for 30 minutes.

8 Next, mix together any remaining dark green and purple buttercream and spread roughly over the board. Swirl in a little of the reserved red buttercream. Next, colour a small amount of the almond paste black and a small amount brown. Roll all the black and brown out into circles, then roll out two white almond paste circles. Use to make the eyes. Alternatively, add a dot of red food colouring paste to make the eyes. Make large teeth with the undyed almond paste and stick on to the jaw.

9 Leave the dinosaur to dry for at least 3 hours before serving.

Centre spine

If you have any of the brighter green left once you have piped the whole body, then pipe on a thin line running from the tip of the tail to the top of the head, running along the centre of the dinosaur body.

Raspberry Ripple Cupcakes

Makes 9

Preparation time: 30 minutes
Cooking time: 20 minutes, plus cooling

50g/2oz seedless raspberry
    jam (jelly)
50g/2oz/scant ½ cup fresh
    raspberries
125g/4oz/1 stick unsalted butter,
    softened
100g/3½oz/scant ½ cup caster
    sugar
2 medium (US large) eggs
1 tbsp milk
150g/5oz/1 cup self-raising
    (self-rising) flour, sifted

For the topping and decoration:
150g/5oz/1¼ cups fresh
    raspberries
300ml/10fl oz/1¼ cups whipping
    cream
50g/2oz/½ cup icing
    (confectioners') sugar, sifted

Piping (decorating) bag
    and star nozzle (tip)

PER CUPCAKE: 385 cals; 26g fat (of which 16g saturates); 36g carbohydrate; 0.5g salt

1 Preheat the oven to 190°C (170°C fan oven)/375ºF/Gas mark 5. Line a 12-hole muffin tin (pan) with 9 paper muffin cases (liners).

2 Mix the raspberry jam (jelly) with the 50g/2oz/scant ½ cup of raspberries, lightly crushing the raspberries. Set aside.

3 Using a hand-held electric whisk, whisk the butter and caster sugar in a bowl, or beat with a wooden spoon, until pale and creamy **2**. Gradually whisk in the eggs and milk until just combined. Using a metal spoon, fold in the flour until just combined, then carefully fold in the raspberry jam (jelly) mixture until just marbled, being careful not to over-mix. Divide the mixture equally among the paper cases.

4 Bake for 20 minutes or until golden and risen. Cool in the tin for 5 minutes, then transfer to a wire rack and leave to cool completely.

5 For the decoration, reserve 9 raspberries. Mash the remaining raspberries in a bowl with a fork. Pass through a sieve into a bowl to remove the seeds. Using a hand-held electric whisk, whip the cream and icing (confectioners') sugar together until stiff peaks form. Mix the raspberry purée into the cream until combined.

6 Insert a star nozzle (tip) into a piping (decorating) bag, then fill the bag **21** with the cream and pipe a swirl **22** on to the top of each cake. Decorate each with a raspberry.

Modelling

Models can be made in sugarpaste, flowerpaste or almond paste (marzipan) and this section also includes making crystallized flowers and leaves. Some of these decorations can be made several weeks in advance and brought out to be placed on the cake when needed.

Modelling with sugarpaste

Sugarpaste (gumpaste) can be moulded or rolled thinly and dries without cracking. Fully dried decorations will keep indefinitely if packed carefully in an airtight container – use bubble wrap or tissue paper to prevent breakages. Sugarpaste can be bought in a variety of colours or homemade sugarpaste can be dyed – if dyeing, add minute amounts of food colouring (pastes are ideal) with the tip of a cocktail stick and knead in before adding any more.

Before using sugarpaste for modelling, always knead it well to soften and smooth. A little hard white vegetable smeared on the surface of your fingers will stop sugarpaste sticking without the paste drying out. Wrap any sugarpaste you are not using in cling film (plastic wrap) to stop it drying out.

Edible glue

Widely available from all specialist cake shops or via websites, edible glue is suitable for all sugarcraft purposes – especially when modelling figures and making flowers.

Gum tragacanth

Available from specialist cake shops or via websites, gum tragacanth is a natural gum that strengthens many types of icing. A little of it kneaded in (follow the directions on the pot) will make sugarpaste (gumpaste) easier to handle – it will roll thinner without tearing, model without cracking and dry faster and more firmly. Once the gum has been added, wrap the sugarpaste well in cling film (plastic wrap) and let it rest for at least an hour before using. Sugarpaste with gum tragacanth added can be used for very delicate modelling work, which would normally require expensive flowerpaste.

Modelling flowers

Sugar flowers were once moulded by hand and required considerable expertise, but now flower, petal and leaf cutters are available for almost every variety of flower and give lifelike results. Try to have a picture of the real flower in front of you when modelling so you can make your flower as lifelike as possible. Wired flowers can be bound together into sprays.

28 Blossom plunger cutter flowers

1 Buy or colour sugarpaste (gumpaste) to your desired shade. Using an acrylic rolling pin, roll out the sugarpaste very thinly so you can almost see through it.

2 Using a small, medium or large plunger blossom cutter, cut out blossom shapes. Eject the flower (by pressing the plunger) onto a piece of foam pad, then press the centre with a round bone tool (or your little finger) to bend it slightly inwards.

3 If the blossoms need stamens, make a pinhole in the centre of each. Leave to dry. Brush the back of the blossoms with a little blob of edible glue, then thread a stamen through (making sure the head nestles in the cup of the blossom).

29 Wiring blossoms into sprays

You will need about a 10cm/4in length of 28–30 gauge florist's wire and tape. It looks more realistic to make up the sprays with different-sized blossoms.

1 Make a small hook at one end of the wire. Put the stamen of a blossom through the loop and squeeze together to secure. Attach florist's tape as close to the base of the blossom as possible, then twist the wire in your fingers (spiralling down the tape as you do so), to cover about 1cm/½in of the wire and stamen with the tape.

2 Hold another blossom flush against the wire and continue to tightly wrap the tape to join the blossoms securely. When you have added as many blossoms as you want, continue to wrap the tape around the remaining wire stem to neaten.

3 Store flower sprays interleaved with tissue paper in a cardboard box in a cool, dry place.

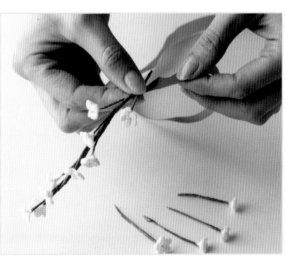

30 Moulding a rose

There are many techniques for making moulded sugar roses – the one detailed here is readily achievable and does not require specialist petal cutters.

1 Use sugarpaste (gumpaste) in your desired shade. Make a cone for the centre of the rose and as base while modelling. Take a pea-sized amount of sugarpaste and shape into a petal in your palm, making it thicker at the base and finer at the rounded top edge. Wrap the first petal, thicker-part down, around the top part of your cone to make the rose bud – the lower part of the cone will later be cut off.

2 Make another petal and position so the centre overlaps the join of the first. Press one side onto the bud and leave the other slightly lifted off. Make a third petal slightly larger than the first two and attach by tucking it inside the lifted part of the second petal. Press gently around the bud at the base and bend the petals over a little at the top to give movement.

3 When the rose is the desired size, cut at the base of the petals and place on a piece of foam pad to dry for at least 24–48 hours.

4 When dry, attach to your cake with a small dab of royal icing. For a rose bud, attach fewer petals and keep the tops of the petals tighter.

31 Using petal cutters

You will need: sifted cornflour (cornstarch) or icing (confectioners') sugar, petal paste in shades of pink, small, medium and large rose-petal cutters, cocktail stick, sponge block.

1   Lightly dust the work surface with cornflour (cornstarch) or icing (confectioners') sugar. Using the pale pink for the outer petals, roll out a small piece of sugarpaste very thinly.

2   Dust the petal cutters with sugar and cut 3–4 petals in various sizes. Gently roll a cocktail stick over the round edge of the petal for a thinner frilled edge. Repeat using the small cutters and a darker shade of paste for inner petals. To make rose buds, cut out small petals in different shades.

3   Place each petal on the sponge block and gently curl to give a shallow cup shape. Curl the petals for the centre of the rose into cones. Cover each petal loosely with cling film to stop it drying out. Assemble the rose as above.

Leaves

Lightly dust the work surface as before, roll out the sugarpaste (gumpaste) thinly and stamp out shapes with a leaf cutter (plunge cutters will imprint veins onto the leaf). Alternatively, use a small knife and imprint the veins manually. Allow the leaves to dry flat on baking parchment, or bend over a piece of dowel or crumpled foil to give movement.

Daisy

Roll out light pink, yellow or white sugarpaste (gumpaste) into small rectangles. Make a line of snips along one long edge, fan out the snips and flatten lightly. Brush the un-snipped edge of the rectangle with water and roll up. Fan out the petals and lightly squeeze the unsnipped base to secure. Press a small ball of yellow sugarpaste into the centre, and attach a sturdy green sugarpaste stalk, if desired. Leave to dry before using.

32 Moulding animals

Let your imagination run wild – it will help you to create fabulous real and mythical creatures. Use a little water or edible glue to stick the pieces together.

Mouse

1   Roll some white sugarpaste (gumpaste) into a pear shape for the body. Roll two small balls and flatten for the ears. Using scissors or a cocktail stick, snip or press whiskers into the icing.

2   Roll two small balls of pink sugarpaste and flatten them. Attach to the white ears with a little water or edible glue. Pinch the base of the ears together and press into the mouse at either side of the head (use a cocktail stick to help you).

3   Roll a length of sugarpaste into a tail and attach to the mouse with a little water or edible glue. Pipe on the eyes.

Duck

1   Take a marble-size piece of yellow sugarpaste (gumpaste) and roll it into a ball. Flatten slightly between thumb and index finger to make the head.

2   Using some more yellow sugarpaste, mould a larger pear shape to make the body. Pinch the tapered end upwards to make the duck's tail.

3   If you like, using a pair of scissors, snip both sides of the duck (with the tip of the scissors facing the head) and pinch the cuts out to make wings.

4   Take a tiny amount of orange sugarpaste and mould into a beak with a rounded, rather than pointy, end. Attach to the head, then pipe on the eyes.

Penguin

1   Take a piece of black sugarpaste (gumpaste) and roll it into an egg shape. Roll a small piece of white sugarpaste into a ball and flatten into an oval. Stick the oval to the front of the penguin's body.

2   Roll a small piece of black sugarpaste into a ball and place on top of the body to make the head. Using a cocktail stick, make two small holes for the eyes. Shape a small piece of orange sugarpaste into a cone shape and press gently on to the head to form a beak.

3   Squeezing small bits of black sugarpaste between your fingers will give you wing shapes – attach these to the body. Using the orange icing, make two small flattish ovals and attach to the base of the body to make the feet.

4   To make a scarf, roll out a piece of contrasting-coloured icing, cut into a long strip and wrap around the penguin's neck. To make a hat, mould a cone and attach to the penguin's head. For buttons, roll icing into small balls. Leave to dry completely.

5   Attach to cakes with buttercream or royal icing.

Ladybird, tortoise and hedgehog

1   Roll out red sugarpaste (gumpaste) thinly for the ladybird (ladybug), and green for the tortoise. Use to cover cold cake buns. Cover another bun with chocolate buttercream for the hedgehog, shaping it to form a snout.

2   Using black writing icing, pipe wings, spots and a smile on the ladybirds and use chocolate drops for eyes.

3   Use brown writing icing to draw 'shell' markings and add white chocolate drops on the tortoise. Make the head, legs and tail from brown icing, and attach to the body with a little jam (jelly). Add silver balls for eyes.

4   Decorate the hedgehog with chocolate sprinkles, silver or gold balls for eyes and a dolly mixture sweet (candy) for the nose.

33 Christmas decorations

Christmas can make even the most terrified sugarcrafter try their hand at this skill. Here are a few easy ideas to get you started. Dust your work surface with sifted icing (confectioners') sugar or cornflour (cornstarch) to stop the sugarpaste (gumpaste) from sticking, then, using an acrylic rolling pin, roll out sugarpaste to a 3mm/⅛in thickness.

Using Christmas cookie cutters (such as stars, bells, trees, reindeers, and so on), stamp out shapes and brush the underside with water. Position on your sugarpasted cake and gently press into place. Alternatively, leave the shapes to dry on a sheet of baking parchment, then rest them on the sides and top of the cake.

Christmas snowman

1 Shape three ever-decreasing balls of white sugarpaste (gumpaste). Fix the middle ball on top of the largest ball with a little edible glue, to make a body. Now glue the smallest ball to the body to make the head.

2 Using tiny beads of black sugarpaste, make three 'coal' buttons and fix down the middle of the centre white ball. Now fix two black beads in place for the eyes, and more to make a smile (spacing the beads a little way apart to resemble coal).

3 Using some coloured sugarpaste (red or green are particularly Christmassy), shape a cone for the snowman's hat and a strip for the scarf. Stick two small twigs or cocktail sticks into the central white ball to make the arms. Leave to dry before using.

Christmas holly and berries

You will need: icing (confectioners') sugar, red and green ready-made fondant icing, holly leaf cutter, cocktail stick, royal icing.

1 Lightly dust a work surface with icing (confectioners') sugar. Roll out the green icing thinly. Cut out holly leaves with the cutter.

2 Using a cocktail stick, mark a central vein down the middle of the leaf, with smaller veins marked off at an angle.

3 Twist the leaves slightly to make a holly leaf shape and dry over the handle of a wooden spoon for 24 hours to create a curved shape.

4 Roll out berries from the red icing. Fix the leaves and berries to your cake with a blob of royal icing.

White and gold Christmas holly

1   Use white ready-made fondant icing to cut out the holly leaves and proceed as on page 89.

2   Dip the edges of the leaves in edible gold glitter or gold leaf to finish.

Christmas rose

You will need: sifted cornflour (cornstarch) and icing (confectioners') sugar, petal paste, medium rose-petal cutter, sponge block, yellow dusting powder, stamens, fine paintbrushes.

1   Lightly dust the work surface with cornflour (cornstarch) or icing (confectioners') sugar. Roll out a small piece of petal paste very thinly. Keep the rest of the paste covered with cling film (plastic wrap).

2   Dust the petal cutter with sugar and cut out 5 petals. Gently roll a cocktail stick over the round edge of the petal to make a thinner, slightly frilled edge.

3   Place each petal on the sponge block and gently curl each one to give a shallow cup shape. Cover each petal loosely with cling film to stop it drying out.

4   Brush one side of the first petal with water, then put the next petal in position, overlapping the edges. Repeat, adding two more petals.

5   Dust your fingers with sugar or cornflour and cup the half-assembled flower. Put the last petal in position so that it overlaps the fourth petal and tucks under the first to form a rose. Leave to dry for 1 hour.

6   Using a dry brush, dust the insides of the flower with yellow dusting powder, brushing from the centre outwards for a graduated effect.

7   Using the end of a teaspoon, put a blob of royal icing in the centre of the flower. Cut 4–5 stamens in half to make 8–10 heads, trim to size and position in the icing.

34 Modelling with a template

1 Trace the design onto greaseproof (wax) paper, dividing it into sections if necessary. Select colours for the design; alternatively, cut out in white sugarpaste (gumpaste) and paint the pieces with food colours.

2 Dust your work surface with sifted icing (confectioners') sugar or cornflour (cornstarch) to stop the sugarpaste sticking, then use an acrylic rolling pin to roll out your first colour thinly. Put the template on top of the sugarpaste and, using a scribing needle or pin, mark the outline of the relevant shape.

3 Using a small sharp knife or scalpel, cut out the design pieces. Repeat until all the elements have been cut out.

4 Assemble the pieces to make sure they fit, then apply them piece by piece onto the iced cake – take care not to over-handle or mis-shape the pieces. Secure the design to the cake using a little egg white or edible glue. Alternatively, allow the pieces to dry (in the correct shape) on a sheet of baking parchment before fixing to your cake.

35 Sugarpaste frills

Layers of fine sugarpaste (gumpaste) frills cascading down the sides of a cake can look spectacular. They can be attached as a single layer or in many layers in scalloped or arched designs. Ideally, use sugarpaste strengthened with gum tragacanth (see page 82).

1 Dust your work surface with sifted icing (confectioners') sugar or cornflour (cornstarch) to stop the sugarpaste sticking, then, using an acrylic rolling pin, roll out the sugarpaste thinly.

2 Cut out the desired shape using a circular frill cutter, or cut a narrow plain or scalloped strip, and place on a flat surface. Dip a cocktail stick into icing sugar or cornflour and roll it backwards and forwards along a short section of the edge of the sugarpaste until the edge begins to frill. Move along until it is all frilled.

3 If using a circular frill cutter, slice the frill open with a knife and ease it to the shape of your cake. Attach to the cake with royal icing. Apply some coloured or lustre dust to your frills, if you like.

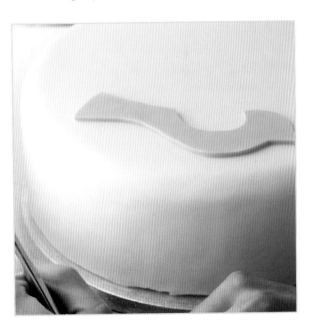

36 Modelling with flowerpaste

Sugar flowerpaste is ideal for making ultra-fine decorations like flowers, leaves, bows and frills, as well as intricate plaques (plaque cutters of varying shapes and sizes are available). Flowerpaste is easy (almost elastic) to handle and sets incredibly hard without becoming too brittle – in its dried state it is often mistaken for porcelain.

Flowerpaste can be bought in small sachets or tubs from cake specialist shops or via websites, but is fairly expensive. Alternatively, you can try making your own – liquid glucose and gum tragacanth are available from all cake icing and decorating specialists. Only use liquid or powder food colouring to colour flowerpaste or it will not dry properly.

Flowerpaste daisy

1 Lightly dust the work surface with sifted icing (confectioners') sugar. Using an acrylic rolling pin, roll out some white flowerpaste thinly, using a little white fat if necessary to stop it sticking. Using a daisy cutter, cut out the shape. Use a modelling knife or scalpel to cut each petal in half to double the number of petals (make sure the daisy is not sticking to the surface).

2 Using a cocktail stick, lightly roll the tip of each petal on a flat surface, to frill it slightly, put on to a piece of foam pad and press the centre of each with a round bone tool (or your little finger) to bend it slightly inwards.

Makes 350g/12oz flowerpaste

225g/8oz/heaping 1¾ cups icing (confectioners' sugar, plus extra to dust, 1 tbsp gum tragacanth, 1 rounded tsp liquid glucose, 1–2 tbsp cold water

1 Sift the icing (confectioners') sugar and gum tragacanth into a bowl. Make a well in the centre and add the liquid glucose and 1 tbsp water. Mix together with your finger to form a soft paste, adding a touch more water as necessary. Knead on a work surface dusted lightly with sifted icing sugar until smooth, white and free from cracks.

2 Put into a polythene bag or wrap in cling film (plastic wrap) to exclude air. Leave to rest for 2 hours before use, then re-knead. Use small pieces at a time, making sure the remaining flowerpaste is tightly wrapped to stop it drying out.

3 Make a small hook in the end of a short length of 26-gauge florist's (covered) wire. Dip the hook end in edible glue, then cover the hook with a small bead of yellow flowerpaste. If you want, repaint the beads with glue and dip into pollen dust. Push the wire through the daisy so that the centre nestles into the inward bend of the daisy. Brush the underside with edible glue to secure.

4 Using the cutter provided, cut out the calyx (the fine greenish petals at the base of the flower) from thinly rolled green flowerpaste, or shape using your fingers. Thread on to the back of the daisy and secure with some more edible glue. Leave the daisy to dry on a piece of foam pad (pricking the wire into the foam so that the daisy doesn't bend).

5 To make the flower ever more special, brush the base of the petals with moss green coloured dust. If you want, combine the daisies into sprays **29**.

37 Modelling with almond paste

Almond paste (marzipan) can be used to model decorations such as flowers, fruit and figurines, which are ideal for adding interest to birthday, novelty or individual cakes.

Almond paste generally only comes in white or yellow; to colour it, dip the tip of a cocktail stick into the desired shade of food colouring paste and smear onto the almond paste. Start with a little first, as you can always add more. Knead until the desired shade is achieved (dust your hands with icing (confectioners') sugar to stop any sticking). When you have the desired shade, knead a small amount until soft and pliable, then roll or mould into shapes. Allow at least 24 hours drying time for almond paste shapes, so the oil in the mixture will not soak into the iced cake.

Carrots

1 Knead 65g/2½oz almond paste until pliable. Add a dab of orange food colouring paste and knead evenly until distributed. Divide into 15 evenly sized pieces and roll each into a small cone. Put the cones on a tray lined with greaseproof (wax) paper or **baking** parchment.
2 Mark ridges down the top and sides of each cone to give the carrot life. Use a small amount of green almond paste or chopped angelica to make the top of the carrot.

Fruit

Lemon – Mould yellow almond paste into a plump oval. Roll over the fine surface of a grater to give a lemon peel texture. Press in a clove at one end for the stalk, or use some brown almond paste. Use green almond paste to shape into a leaf.

Orange – Roll orange almond paste into balls. Using a cocktail stick, mark the skin to give texture. Add green almond paste leaves.

Pineapple – Roll yellow almond paste into a plump oval. Mark a criss-cross pattern. Shape a small rectangle in green almond paste and snip along one edge. Carefully round the snips (without tearing them off the base) to make the pineapple top. Attach to the pineapple base.

Strawberry – Shape red almond paste into a rounded cone and roll over the medium-coarse surface of a grater. Shape green almond paste to form the hull (or use a suitably-shaped plunger cutter).

Grapes – Use pale green and mauve almond paste. Shape the green into a cone and flatten slightly. Roll small balls of mauve almond paste for grapes and stick to the flattened cone. Add a green vine leaf.

Apple – Roll pale green almond paste into a ball. Press a clove into the top, or use some brown almond paste.

38 Moulding figures

Moulding figures requires care and patience. They need two key factors to make them come alive: one is proportion and the other facial expression. With practise, you'll learn the feel of the moulding material and how much pressure to apply.

Use sugarpaste (gumpaste) (ideally strengthened with gum tragacanth – see page 82) or almond paste for figure modelling. Most figures are made from three basic shapes: a ball for the head, a sausage for the body, and pears for the limbs. Body parts are often moulded separately, left to dry and then assembled. Always gauge the size of your figures in relation to the cake and factor in the drying time.

Almond paste is used for figures that need to be sturdy and stand upright. It is firm and easy to work with, although the texture is slightly grainy in comparison to sugarpaste. Make sure you allow at least 24 hours drying time for almond paste figures so that the oil in the mixture will not soak into the iced cake. Sugarpaste is used for delicate figures and finer work. It can be made wafer thin without cracking and dries solid (after many days).

Modelling tools are available to shape and mark patterns; however, there will be lots of kitchen utensils in your drawers that will do similar jobs – wooden skewers, small spatulas and small sharp knives are all useful. It's a good idea to invest in a fine brush for painting features using food colouring pastes. If applying colourings directly on to models, ensure the figures are dry first.

Wrestler

1 Roll a ball of flesh-coloured sugarpaste (gumpaste) or almond paste for the head. Roll a long sausage of the same colour for the arms. Use your little finger to mark muscle definition and flatten each end to make hands. Add finger definition with a knife or cocktail stick. Roll out two flesh-coloured sturdy legs, marking the muscles.

2 Shape some contrasting-coloured almond paste or sugarpaste into the trunk of the body, making it 'v' shaped where the legs will join.

3 Make two boots: they need to match the width of the base of the legs where they will join, and be quite solid and flat so that the figure will stand.

4 Firmly press the arms to the top of the body. Cut the top of the legs at an angle and press to the base of the body (on the sides of the 'v'). Press the boots on to the base of the legs. Put on to baking parchment to dry (lying down).

5 When dry, thinly roll out some more coloured almond paste or sugarpaste and cut strips for the straps of the wrestler suit. Position over the shoulders. Using food colouring pastes, paint in the eyes and a mouth. Shape a little brown or yellow almond paste or sugarpaste to make the hair and moustache. Attach to the head.

39 Crystallizing flowers and leaves

Edible flowers make a stunning individual decoration for cupcakes or clustered en masse on celebration cakes: rose petals and buds, daisies, pansies, violas and lavender sprigs are all suitable. Herbs, such as rosemary and mint, bay leaves and sweet geranium leaves and fruit, such as grapes and redcurrants, can also be crystallized. They will keep for up to a week in a cool, dry place. Always use flowers and leaves that have not been sprayed with chemicals.

1 Lightly beat an egg white until slightly frothy. Using a small paintbrush, coat the flowers, leaves or fruit with the egg white.

2 Sprinkle with caster sugar to coat lightly and shake off the excess.

3 Leave to dry on baking parchment for two days in a cool, dry place – an airing cupboard or pantry is ideal – where they will crisp and harden.

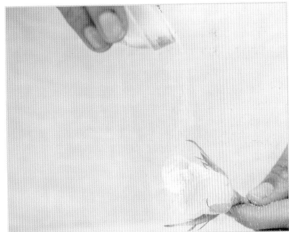

Rosebud Wedding Cake

Cuts into 180–200
small slices

Preparation time: at least 1 day,
plus drying

250g/9oz sugar flowerpaste (from
    cake decorating supplier)
Pink food colouring
5kg/11lb white sugarpaste
    (gumpaste)
White royal icing (see page 33)
    made with 225g/8oz icing
    (confectioners') sugar
1 × 30.5cm/12in round Rich Fruit
    Cake (see pages 24–26) covered
    in almond paste
1 × 23cm/9in round Rich Fruit
    cake (see pages 24–26) covered
    in almond paste
1 × 15cm/6in round Rich Fruit
    cake (see pages 24–26) covered
    in almond paste

40.5cm/16in cake board (drum)
23cm/9in cake board (double
    thick)
15cm/6in cake board (double
    thick)
Piping (decorating) bag and no. 2
    and no. 3 piping nozzles (tips)
6 plastic cake dowels
Pink ribbon
Fresh pink roses (optional)

PER SLICE: 555 cals; 16g fat (of which 5g

saturates); 92g carbohydrate; 0.2g salt

1   To make sugar roses, colour the flowerpaste different shades of pale pink. Make a cone shape a bit smaller than the size of the petal. Roll the flowerpaste out thinly, using only small amounts at a time, and cut out a 5-petal rose shape with a cutter **31**. Thin the edges of the petals slightly with a bone tool, or roll them over a cocktail stick.

2   Dampen the lower part of each petal with a little water and wrap the petals around the cone one at a time, slightly overlapping each petal as you go. Repeat with a second set of 5 petals. Using your fingers, curl the outer edges of the petals to give a natural rose shape. Repeat to make at least 12 roses. Use a smaller cutter to make at least 24 roses for the sides of the cakes. Leave overnight to harden.

3   Place each cake on its cake board. Roll out some sugarpaste (gumpaste) to 4–5mm/¼in thick and large enough to cover the largest cake **11**. Dampen the cake with a little boiled water. Lift the icing on to the cake and smooth over the top and sides, trimming the excess icing away around the base. Dampen the surrounding cake board. Roll out a long thin strip of icing to cover the board **12** and trim away the excess. Ice the two smaller tiers in the same way.

4   Cut a circle of greaseproof (wax) paper to the size of the top of each cake **24**. Fold the largest two into 8 segments, the smallest into 6 segments. Using a compass or the bottom of a glass with the right diameter, pencil a scallop on the rounded edge between the folds about 5cm/2in deep for the larger cakes and 2.5cm/1in deep for the top tier. Cut out the scallops.

5   Open out the paper and place the smallest piece in the centre of the smallest cake and the two larger pieces in the centre of the two larger cakes. Hold the paper with one hand while pricking the scalloped outline on to the icing.

6   For the side scallops, cut a strip of greaseproof paper the circumference of the cake. As before, fold into 8 segments and mark the scallops in the same way. Remove the paper and, using a piping (decorating) bag fitted with the plain no. 3 nozzle (tip) and filled with white royal icing **21**, pipe a line of icing along the line of the scallops **22**. Leave to dry for about 1 hour before piping a second, thinner line on top of the first using the no. 2 nozzle.

7   Push three dowels into each of the two larger cakes **19**. Using a pencil, mark the dowels where they are level with the top of the cake. Remove the dowels and cut each one where marked. However, if the top of the cake is not completely flat, make sure the three dowels are cut to equal length otherwise the cake above may slope. Push the dowels back into the holes. Carefully stack the middle and top cakes.

8   Secure a piece of ribbon around each cake with a small dot of royal icing **15**.

9   Complete the decoration by piling up the large icing roses on the centre of the top cake and placing a smaller rose at each of the points where the scallops meet. Surround with fresh roses and petals, if you like.

Baby Bunny Christening Cake

Cuts into about 36 slices

To decorate: 1½ hours

About 500g/1lb 2oz white
   sugarpaste (gumpaste)
Yellow and blue food colouring
   pastes
Icing (confectioners') sugar, sifted,
   to dust
1 × 18cm/7in square Rich Fruit
   Cake (see pages 24–26),
   almond-pasted **9** and
   sugarpasted (gumpasted) **11**
   on a cake board
White royal icing (see page 33)
   made with 225g/8oz/1¾ cups
   icing (confectioners') sugar
Alphabet letter sweets (candies)
   (optional)

Piping (decorating) bag and
   star nozzle (tip)

PER SLICE: 395 cals; 11g fat (of which 4.5g

saturates); 75g carbohydrate; 0.2g salt

Spare sugarpaste

Remember to always keep
any sugarpaste (gumpaste)
not in use covered with cling
film (plastic wrap) to stop it
drying out.

1 Colour 75g/3oz white sugarpaste (gumpaste)pale yellow and shape some of it into an oval body **32**. Next, mould a slightly squashed round and, using water fix on to the body to make the bunny's head. Using a cocktail stick, press in holes to mark the eyes and pinch out a little icing to make the nose.

2 Using a little more of the yellow sugarpaste, mould and attach two arms to the body and two legs at the base, with flattened ovals for the feet. Use the remaining yellow sugarpaste to form the ears. Roll out a little white sugarpaste and cut out 2 small teardrop shapes to decorate the bunny ears. Fix to the ears with a little water, then fix the ears to the bunny head. Roll out a small amount of the white sugarpaste to make the mouth. Roll out a circle of white sugarpaste and stick onto the body. Add a small circle of white sugarpaste to each foot.

3 Colour half the remaining sugarpaste very pale blue. Lightly dust a work surface with icing (confectioners') sugar and roll out a small piece of the blue icing, then cut a small strip and make a bow to decorate the bunny's front. Fix in position with a little water.

4 Reroll the trimmings and roll out another small piece of blue icing to look like a blanket. Place on top of the cake and sit the bunny in the centre of the blanket. Leave to dry in position.

5 Roll out a little more of the blue sugarpaste and cut out an 18cm/7in long, 2.5cm/1in wide strip. Make sure the strip is lying flat, then roll a cocktail stick backwards and forwards across a short section of the edge until it frills **35**. Repeat along the whole length of the strip. Attach the strip with a little water to one of the top edges of the cake, so that the frill sticks above the level of the icing. Repeat with the remaining three edges.

6 Colour the remaining white sugarpaste pale yellow. Roll out sections of yellow and blue icing to about 3mm/⅛in thick. Cut out rough 2.5cm/1in squares (they don't need to be very accurate). Press each square gently on to the surface of a grater, to give texture. Brush a section of the side of the cake (starting at the base) with water, and stick on squares in alternating colours. Carry on until all the sides are covered (you might need to colour some more icing depending on the depth of your cake/thickness of the squares).

7 To decorate the base of the cake, fit a piping (decorating) bag with a star nozzle (tip) and fill with white royal icing **21** . Hold the piping bag straight above the surface, with the nozzle just touching the surface. Press out some icing until you have the size of the star you want **22**, meanwhile lifting the bag slightly to give the star space. Stop pressing, then pull up sharply to break the icing. Repeat next to the first star all around the cake to make a border.

8 Use alphabet letter sweets (candies), if you like, to write the baby's name on top of the cake and stick them on with a little water. Leave to dry.

Toadstool

Cuts into 12 slices

Preparation time: 1½ hours
Cooking time: 40 minutes,
plus cooling

Unsalted butter to grease
1 × 3-egg quantity of Victoria
    Sponge mixture (see page 22)
700g/1½lb white sugarpaste
    (gum paste)
Brown, red, green and yellow
    food colourings
½ × quantity of buttercream
    (see page 32)
Cornflour (cornstarch) to dust
Sugar flowers, dolly mixture
    sweets (candies) and
    butterfly decorations

1 large rectangular cake board
Piping (decorating) bag and
    small, fluted nozzle (tip)

PER SLICE: 433 cals; 10g fat (of which 6g
saturates); 87g carbohydrate; 0.3g salt

1 Preheat the oven to 190°C (170°C fan oven)/375°F/Gas mark 5.
Grease a 900g/2lb food can and a 1.1 litre/2¼ pint pudding basin and
base-line **1** with baking parchment. It doesn't matter how big the basin
is, as long as it holds at least 1.1 litres/2¼ pints. A wide, shallow cake
makes a better-looking toadstool.

2 Make the cake mixture according to the instructions on page 22. Half-
fill the food can and put the remaining mixture into the pudding basin.
Bake for about 30 minutes for the 'stalk' in the food can and 40 minutes
for the 'mushroom cap' in the pudding basin **3** . Transfer both to a wire
rack and leave to cool.

3 Take 350g/12oz sugarpaste (gumpaste). Colour a walnut-sized piece
with brown food colouring and the rest red. Colour 125g/4oz green and
leave the remaining 225g/8oz white. Roll out the green icing and cut into
a kidney shape as a 'grass' base. Fix to a cake board with a little water
12. Unmould the cakes. Using the food can that the stalk was baked
in as a template, cut a semi-circle from one side of the grass.

4 Reserve 50g/2oz white icing. Colour the rest yellow and roll out into
a long oblong to fit the stalk. Trim the edges. Spread buttercream **5**
thinly around the stalk cake then, holding the cake by the ends, set it at
one end of the icing. Roll up the icing around the stalk and press the seam
together. With a dab of buttercream, fix the stalk upright in the cut-out
semi-circle in the green icing. Spread the top with buttercream.

5 Roll out the red icing to fit the mushroom cap. Set the cake flat on the
work surface. Cover the upper surface thinly with buttercream. Lay the
red icing over the cake **11**. Smooth in place and trim around the base.
Dust the work surface lightly with cornflour (cornstarch) and carefully
turn the cake upside down.

6 Colour the remaining buttercream dark brown. Insert a small,
fluted nozzle (tip) into a piping (decorating) bag. Fill the bag with the
buttercream **21**. Mark a circle in the centre of the base of the mushroom
cap, where the stalk will fit. Pipe lines **22** of buttercream radiating from
this, to look like the 'gills' of a toadstool. Cover the sponge and red icing
join. Turn the cake the right way up and set on top of the stalk. Roll out
the reserved white icing and the brown icing. Cut the white icing into
dots. Arrange on top of the toadstool, using buttercream to fix them. Cut
the brown icing into windows and a door and fix to the stalk in the same
way. Decorate the 'grass' with flowers, sweets (candies) and butterflies.

Handbag Cake

Cuts into about 16 slices

Preparation time: 1½ hours
Cooking time: about 1 hour, plus cooling, setting and drying

2 × baked Marble Cakes (see page 30)
500g/1lb 2oz vanilla or chocolate buttercream (see page 32)
Icing (confectioners') sugar, sifted, to dust
About 800g/1lb 12oz white sugarpaste (gumpaste)
Yellow (or gold) and black food colourings
Gold lustre dust
Silver balls (optional)

1 × medium round cake board

PER SLICE: 686 cals; 32g fat (of which 17g saturates); 101g carbohydrate; 0.9g salt

Colour and design

Use any design or colour you like to transform this cake into a fashionista's dream. Always keep any sugarpaste not in use covered with cling film (plastic wrap) to stop it drying out.

1 Cut both cooled marble cakes in half horizontally **4**. Put the narrow base section of one of the cakes on a cake board. Spread some buttercream over the top, then lay on the wider top, cut-side down. Ice the top of the reassembled cake with more buttercream. Next, lay on the wider top section of the other cake, cut side up. Spread over some more buttercream, then top with the remaining narrow base section, cut side down. Your large cake should have a slight diamond shape.

2 If you want, carve the cake into more of a handbag shape, then spread any remaining buttercream lightly over the cake **5** and leave to set for 30 minutes.

3 Lightly dust a work surface with icing (confectioners') sugar and roll out 500g/1lb 2oz white sugarpaste (gumpaste) until it's large enough to cover the cake. With the help of the rolling pin, lift the icing on to the cake and smooth down **11**. Trim away any excess icing.

4 Next, tint 75g/3oz white sugarpaste yellow (or as close to gold as you can get it). Roll out 50g/2oz and cut into a strip about 25.5cm/10in long and 2.5cm/1in wide. Use a knife, cocktail stick or crimpers to mark a zip pattern along the centre of the strip and stitch marks along the edges. Brush the strip with gold lustre dust. Add the trimmings to the remaining yellow sugarpaste and roll into one large and one small rectangle, to make the clasp, and four small squares, to make the handle fastenings. Use a knife, cocktail stick or crimpers to mark stitch marks around the squares. Brush with gold lustre. Reroll the trimmings into piping for the flap. Put all to one side.

5 Dye the remaining sugarpaste black. Attach the zip to the top of the cake with a little boiled and cooled water. Shape a little of the black sugarpaste into two small triangles or rectangles and fix one to each end of the zip, using water and pressure. If you like, press some silver balls on to the black ends of the zip for added glitz.

6 Lightly dust a work surface with icing (confectioners') sugar and roll out some more of the black sugarpaste until it is about 5mm/¼in thick. Cut into a rounded, tapered square to make the closing flap. Using a knife, cocktail stick or crimpers, add some marks around the edges to look like stitching, then lay the flap over the centre of the zip. Fix the two gold rectangles in place to make the clasp, using water and pressure. If you like, add silver balls to the clasp as rivets.

7 Roll out the remaining black sugarpaste and cut out two strips for the handles. Place over the flap and secure each end with a yellow square handle fastening. If you like, press a silver ball into the middle of each square. Attach the yellow piping to the flap, using water and pressure.

8 Roll out the black sugarpaste trimmings thinly and cut out zebra-pattern shapes. Brush them with gold lustre dust, if you like, and fix to the cake with a little water. Leave to dry before serving.

Jungle Cake

Cuts into about 30 slices

To decorate: 1 hour, plus drying

20.5cm/8in round Chocolate,
  Madeira or Victoria Sponge
  cake (see pages 23, 29 or 22)
12.5cm/5in round Chocolate,
  Madeira or Victoria Sponge
  cake (see pages 23, 29 or 22)
750g/1lb 1oz buttercream (see
  page 32)
Blue, yellow, pink and black food
  colouring pastes
450g/1lb white almond paste
  (see page 33)
Cocoa powder, sifted
About 50g/2oz each of pink and
  blue sugarpaste (gumpaste)
  (optional)
Icing (confectioners') sugar to dust

Cake board or plate

PER SLICE: 368 cals; 19g fat (of which 11g
saturates); 49g carbohydrate; 0.4g salt

Modelling animals
Using almond paste to
model animals will give them
a more rounded, playful
appearance – ideal for a
child's birthday cake.

1   Split both cakes in half horizontally and use some of the buttercream to sandwich them together **4**. Use a little more buttercream to sandwich the smaller cake on to the larger cake, placing it off-centre. Place the cake on a cake board or plate.

2   Place two-thirds of the remaining buttercream in one bowl, and the remainder in a second bowl. Dye the larger amount of buttercream bright green, using blue and yellow food colouring, then set aside. Take a few tablespoonfuls of buttercream out of the smaller bowl and set aside. Dye the remaining icing in the second bowl bright blue and spread on to the cakes **5** to resemble water cascading down from the top tier. Swirl in a little of the set-aside white buttercream to make the water look more realistic. Dye any remaining white buttercream bright pink and put into a piping (decorating) bag **21** fitted with a small plain nozzle (tip). Spread the green buttercream over the cake, around the water. Swirl the icing as you go.

3   Using a little black food colouring paste, dye 125g/4oz almond paste grey. Use most of this to make the drinking elephant **32**: make an oval for the body and a round head, pinching out the trunk. Attach short sausage shapes for legs and flattened ovals for ears. Roll out two ovals from white almond paste and attach one to each ear with a little water. Position the elephant on the lower tier, with its trunk in the water. Use a cocktail stick to prick two eyes and mark some stripes on the trunk. Use the remaining grey almond paste to make the hippo head: a fat oval with marked eyes, nostrils, mouth and snout. Attach two small ears to the top of the head. Dye a tiny amount of almond paste pink, roll out and attach to the ears. Position the hippo in the water on the top tier, securing the head at an angle on a little more grey almond paste.

4   Dye 40g/1½oz of the remaining almond paste brown with cocoa powder. Set aside a small amount to make the spots on the giraffe. Use the remaining amount to make the monkey: an oval for the body and a round for the head, two longer sausages for the arms and tail, and shorter sausages for the legs. Use a little uncoloured almond paste to put a flattened circle on the front of the stomach and a flattened oval on the bottom half of the face. Use a cocktail stick to mark out eyes and nostrils. Position on the base layer.

5   Dye 65g/2½oz of the remaining almond paste yellow. Use a tiny bit to make a banana **37** for the monkey to hold, and shape the rest into the sitting giraffe: a larger oval for the body and a round with a snout pinched out for the head. Attach two small triangles on top of the head for the ears, and use some of the reserved brown almond paste to make the horns. Shape and attach the legs. Stick on small dots of brown to give the giraffe his spots, and use a cocktail stick to mark the eyes and nostrils. Position on top of the cake, on the grass.

6   Dye a tiny bit of almond paste black for the alligator eyes. Reserve a tiny bit of uncoloured almond paste for teeth. Dye the remaining almond paste green and shape some of it into the alligator heads. Add the eyes and teeth. Position the heads in the water and use a cocktail stick to make lines across the snouts. Lightly dust a work surface with icing (confectioners') sugar, then roll out any remaining green almond paste and cut out leaves – attach these where you want. Using the reserved pink buttercream, pipe **22** pink rosette flowers around the cake. Alternatively, use pink and blue sugarpaste (gumpaste) and a small plunger blossom cutter to cut blossom shapes **28**. Leave to dry.

Using Chocolate and Sugar

Chocolate decorations give an elegant, luxurious finish to cakes and there are many ways in which chocolate can be used, including moulding and piping. Sugar is also a wonderfully versatile ingredient – it can be transformed into crisp praline or delicate spun sugar.

Selecting chocolate

When bitter cocoa beans have been roasted they are cracked and the husks are removed – leaving behind the cocoa nibs. The nibs are ground into a thick paste and processed into cocoa butter and chocolate liquor (not the sweet variety). Different types of chocolate are created, depending on the proportions of cocoa butter and chocolate liquor used.

White chocolate – Made only from cocoa butter and sugar with no addition of chocolate liquor, hence the white colour and sweet flavour.

Plain (semi-sweet) chocolate – Made from cocoa butter and chocolate liquor and sweetened with sugar. For baking and decorations look for a high percentage of cocoa solids (at least 70%). The plainer the chocolate, the harder the texture and the stronger the flavour.

Couverture chocolate – At the top end of the chocolate quality scale and preferred by chefs for confectionery, couverture is made from cocoa butter and chocolate liquor with no added sugar. The end product is a very dark, brittle chocolate suitable only for chocolate work and cooking. This chocolate is ideal for hand-made chocolates, desserts, gâteaux and decorations. It must be tempered **41** before use.

Milk (sweet) chocolate – Made the same way as plain (semi-sweet) chocolate but with the addition of dried milk powder, which gives it a lighter colour and texture and sweeter flavour.

Cocoa – Made from the chocolate liquor that has been pressed and dried to form an unsweetened chocolate powder.

Other less expensive forms of chocolate are made with some of the cocoa butter replaced with vegetable fat, which makes the chocolate softer in texture and lacking in good flavour. There are guidelines for how much cocoa butter can be removed before the substance is no longer called chocolate.

40 Melting chocolate

Care must be taken when melting chocolate since this determines the set appearance of the chocolate, giving it either a smooth glossy finish or a dull streaked appearance. It is very important not to overheat any type of chocolate, or it will seize into an unusable mess. The bowl in which you are melting the chocolate must be clean and dry. Once melted, the chocolate may be used for dipping, coating, spreading, or for cut-out chocolate pieces (use tempered chocolate **41**) and piped decorations. Always choose good-quality chocolate if melted chocolate is being used and set, as the flavour and texture is important.

Melting chocolate over a saucepan

Break or chop the chocolate and put into a heatproof bowl. Set the bowl over a saucepan of barely simmering water (making sure the bowl does not touch the water, but sits above it and that there is no space between the bowl and the saucepan rim). The steam from the water will gently melt the chocolate – stir occasionally to evenly distribute the heat. Do not try to hurry the process or the chocolate might seize and become unworkable.

Melting chocolate in a microwave

Put the broken or chopped chocolate into a microwave-safe bowl. Microwave on full power for 1 minute. Stir, then heat again in 10-second bursts until the chocolate is smooth and melted. If the temperature of the chocolate gets too high, it can seize or will dry with a streaked surface.

If your chocolate has seized, try stirring in a few drops of flavourless vegetable oil.

41 Tempering chocolate

Tempering chocolate is a method of heating and cooling chocolate to particular temperatures that will ensure the chocolate dries with a hard, glossy finish. For best results, chocolate should be tempered before using in moulds or to make decorations. If chocolate is melted without tempering, it will dry dull, grainy and quite soft. If adding chocolate to recipes, then it usually suffices to melt it as normal. Always temper good-quality plain (semi-sweet) or couverture, milk (sweet) or white chocolates. You will need a very accurate and sensitive thermometer – a digital probe one is best.

1   Melt plain (semi-sweet) chocolate using one of the methods described above until it reaches 45°C/113°F. Milk (sweet) and white chocolate should be heated to 43°C/109°F.

2   Cool the chocolate to 27°C/80.6°F, or 25°C/77°F for milk (sweet) or white chocolate, by placing the bowl in a cool water bath (taking care that none of the water gets into the chocolate). Stir to keep the temperature even on cooling. Alternatively, add an additional 20% chopped chocolate to the melted bowl and stir to melt (this is called 'seeding').

3   Before using the chocolate, test that it is ready to use by dipping a metal palette knife (spatula) into it and tapping off the excess. Leave to harden on the palette knife for 5 minutes – it should dry with a shiny appearance. If the chocolate is not shiny, repeat the tempering process.

4   Use to decorate or fill moulds. The temperature of the chocolate should remain between 27°C/80.6°F and 32°C/89.6°F (25°C/77°F and 30°C/86°F for milk (sweet) and white chocolate) while you work.

42 Moulding chocolate

There are a huge number of wonderful chocolate moulds available, from teacups to rabbits and shoes to seashells. Use tempered chocolate for best results.

1   Sturdy paper or silicone cases (liners) make good chocolate moulds.

2   Pour melted tempered chocolate into a clean, dry mould. Turn the mould to coat it evenly with chocolate, then pour out the excess. Chill until set.

3   Repeat the process until you have the desired thickness (see notes). Leave to set, then turn the chocolate out, handling carefully.

4   Alternatively, use a paintbrush to layer the chocolate – dip the brush into the chocolate and paint the inside of the mould. Leave to set, then repeat layering with chocolate until you have achieved the desired thickness.

Notes

- Your mould should not have awkward curves or angles, or you will not be able to release the chocolate from the mould.
- The larger the mould, the thicker the chocolate layer should be.

43 Chocolate for dipping

This is ideal for small sweets (candies), fruit and nuts. Strawberries are particularly good half-dipped in white chocolate.

1 Fully immerse or half-coat your chosen item in melted chocolate. If needed, use a toothpick or a small fork to lift the item out of the chocolate, then shake to remove any excess.

2 Leave to set on a baking tray lined with baking parchment. Trim off any excess cooled chocolate, to neaten, and use.

44 Chocolate wafers

You can make flat or curved wafers in any shape you like. Cut a piece of baking parchment to the desired width and length; alternatively, cut into individual shapes at this stage.

1 Brush the paper evenly with melted chocolate and leave until the chocolate has almost set. Using kitchen scissors (shears) or a knife, cut the chocolate sheet into pieces of the desired size and shape (if not already so).

2 Leave to cool and harden completely on a sheet of greaseproof (wax) paper or baking parchment, either flat or draped over something for curved results. Using your fingers or a metal palette knife, carefully remove the wafers from the paper, handling them as little as possible, and store in the fridge for up to 24 hours.

45 Large chocolate curls

1 Spread melted chocolate in a thin layer on a marble slab or clean work surface. Leave to firm up.

2 Using a sharp, flat-ended blade (such as a metal pastry scraper), push through the chocolate at a 45-degree angle.

3 The size of the curls will be determined by the width of the blade.

46 Chocolate shavings

This is the easiest decoration of all because it doesn't call for melting chocolate. It's ideal for coating the sides and top of cakes. Use chilled chocolate.

1 Hold a chocolate bar upright on a work surface and shave pieces off the edge with a y-shaped vegetable peeler.

2 Alternatively, grate the chocolate against a coarse or medium-coarse grater to make very fine shavings.

47 Chocolate caraque (fine curls)

The temperature of the set chocolate is important – keep testing the edge to see if it's ready.

1 Pour cooled, melted chocolate on to a marble slab or cool work surface. Using a palette knife, spread out the chocolate as evenly as possible to a thickness of 1–2mm/¹⁄₁₆in. Let the chocolate cool to almost setting point.

2 Using a metal pastry scraper or larger cook's knife held at a 45-degree angle against the marble or work surface, pull the blade towards you slowly to roll the chocolate into a cylinder. If the chocolate is too warm it will stick, if it is too cold it will only form shavings.

48 Chocolate leaves

Use unsprayed rose or other non-toxic leaves, such as bay leaves, and wash and dry them first.

1 Using a small paintbrush, coat the shiny sides of the leaves with a layer of cooled, melted chocolate. Spread it right to the edges, but wipe off any chocolate that drips over the edge (as this can make peeling off the chocolate difficult).

2 Leave to set on a baking sheet lined with baking parchment in a cool, dry place. When completely set, carefully peel away the leaves and store the chocolate leaves in the fridge in an airtight container between sheets of greaseproof (wax) paper or baking parchment for up to one month.

49 Chocolate triangles

These can be stored in the fridge in an airtight container between sheets of greaseproof (wax) paper or baking parchment for up to one month.

1 Cut a length of silicone or baking parchment about 5cm/2in wide. Brush with a 1–2mm/¹⁄₁₆in layer of cooled, melted chocolate. Leave to cool to almost setting point.

2 Mark into triangles and leave to set but do not chill. For curved triangles, set the chocolate-coated paper along the length of a rolling pin or similar curved shape.

50 Piped chocolate decorations

Chocolate can be piped into decorative shapes to add to cakes or piped directly onto them. Alternatively, use chocolate and hazelnut spread to pipe borders – it is already an ideal consistency.

1 Draw your design onto a piece of white paper or card. Tape a large piece of baking parchment over it – work on a flat surface where your decorations can be left to dry completely before moving.

2 Fill a greaseproof (wax) paper piping (decorating) bag **21** with melted chocolate that has been allowed to cool and thicken slightly.

3 Holding the bag vertically, snip off the tip to the size of hole required and, using light pressure, pipe the chocolate onto the design. Leave to set completely.

4 If you wish, fill in your design with a different colour of melted and cooled chocolate, then leave to set.

5 Using a metal palette knife (spatula), carefully remove the piped design. Store between sheets of baking parchment in an airtight container in the fridge for up to one month.

Working with sugar

When heating sugar, always do so in a heavy-based saucepan, wear long sleeves and use oven gloves.

51 Caramel decorations

Caramel decorations can be made a few hours in advance and stored in an airtight container – but can turn sticky depending on the atmosphere.

1 Line a baking sheet with lightly oiled greaseproof (wax) paper. Put 200g/7oz/heaping ¾ cup caster sugar into a heavy-based saucepan with 4 tbsp water. Heat gently to dissolve. Bring to the boil, then cook until it turns a medium caramel colour, swirling the pan to mix – it should be the colour of a dulled copper coin. Dip the base of the pan into cold water. Use the caramel immediately before it begins to harden.

2 For caramel flowers, use a fork to drizzle flower shapes onto oiled greaseproof paper.

3 For caramel cages, lightly oil the back of a ladle. Drizzle caramel threads in a criss-cross pattern over the top, finishing with a thread around the rim. Leave to set then carefully remove the cage.

52 Praline

Used as luminous shards or ground into rubble, praline is a cake decorator's dream.

250g/9oz/heaping 1 cup caster sugar
175g/6oz/1¼ cups nuts, such as walnuts or almonds

1 Put the sugar into a pan and warm over gentle heat. Meanwhile, line a baking sheet with greaseproof (wax) paper or baking parchment.

2 Shake the pan gently to help dissolve the sugar, watching carefully when it starts to colour.

3 When the sugar is a dark golden brown, pour in the nuts and stir once with a wooden spoon. Working quickly, pour the praline onto the paper and spread out. Leave to cool for 20 minutes.

4 Break the praline into shards by hitting with a rolling pin. Use as brittle shards, or whiz in a food processor to a fine powder. Perfect for dusting the sides of buttercream-iced cakes.

53 Spun sugar

One of the most attractive sugar decorations, spun sugar is made from light caramel syrup spun into a nest of hair-thin threads. The only equipment you need is a pair of forks, a rolling pin and sheets of paper to catch any drips of syrup.

1   Put the sugar and water into a saucepan, using 200g/7oz/heaping ¾ cup caster sugar per 4 tbsp water. Heat gently until the sugar dissolves.

2   Turn the heat up to bring to the boil. Continue to boil until the sugar caramelizes, swirling the saucepan to mix – you are looking for the colour of a dulled copper coin. Dip the bottom of the saucepan in cold water and leave to cool for 5 minutes.

3   Dip two or more forks, held in one hand, into the caramel. Flick them back and forth over a rolling pin held over the paper in your other hand, so that wispy threads fall over the pin.

4   When the rolling pin is full, carefully slide off the threads. Use immediately, to decorate cakes or desserts.

5   Alternatively, gently form the threads into an open spun sugar ball.

Chocolate Birthday Cake

Cuts into 12 slices

Preparation time: 30 minutes
Cooking time: 1¼ hours,
plus cooling

150ml/5fl oz sunflower oil,
    plus extra to grease
75g/3oz creamed coconut
25g/1oz plain (semi-sweet)
    chocolate, broken into pieces
50g/2oz/½ cup cocoa powder
350g/12oz/2⅓ cups self-raising
    (self-rising) flour
1 tsp baking powder
Pinch of salt
175g/6oz/1 cup light muscovado
    (brown) sugar

For the icing:
350g/12oz plain (semi-sweet)
    chocolate, broken into small
    pieces
150ml/5fl oz double (heavy) cream
White and milk chocolate
    Maltesers to decorate

PER SLICE: 515 cals; 31g fat (of which 15g
saturates); 59g carbohydrate; 0.4g salt

1   Grease a 1.7 litre/3½ pint, 30.5 × 10cm/12 × 4in loaf tin (pan) and then line **1** with greaseproof (wax) paper. Put the coconut into a heatproof bowl, pour on 425ml/14½fl oz boiling water and stir to dissolve. Set aside to cool for 30 minutes.

2   Melt the chocolate **40** in a heatproof bowl set over a pan of gently simmering water, making sure the base of the bowl doesn't touch the water. Stir until smooth, then remove the bowl from the pan and leave to cool slightly. Preheat the oven to 180°C (160°C fan oven)/350°F/Gas mark 4.

3   Sift the cocoa powder, flour, baking powder and salt into a bowl. Stir in the sugar and make a well in the middle. Add the coconut mixture, melted chocolate and oil and beat to make a smooth batter **2**. Pour the cake batter into the prepared tin.

4   Bake for 1–1¼ hours or until risen and just firm to the touch **3** (if necessary, after about 40 minutes, lightly cover the top of the cake with foil if it appears to be browning too quickly). Leave in the tin for 10 minutes, then transfer to a wire rack and leave to cool completely. When cold, trim to neaten the edges.

5   To make the icing, put the chocolate into a heatproof bowl. Heat the cream to just below boiling point. Pour on to the chocolate and stir until melted. Leave to cool, beating occasionally, until thick – pop into the fridge for 30 minutes to help thicken, if necessary.

6   Cut the cold cake in half horizontally **4** and sandwich the layers together with one-third of the icing. Spread the rest evenly over the top and sides of the cake. Decorate the top of the cake with alternate rows of milk and white Maltesers. Lay an edging of alternate milk and white Maltesers around the base of the cake to decorate.

Egg
free

Easter Chocolate Fudge Cake

Cuts into 12 slices

Preparation time: 30 minutes
Cooking time: 50 minutes, plus cooling

175g/6oz/1½ sticks unsalted
    butter, softened, plus extra
    to grease
150g/5oz/1 cup plain (all-purpose)
    flour
50g/2oz/½ cup cocoa powder
1 tsp baking powder
Pinch of salt
150g/5oz/heaping ¾ cup light
    muscovado (brown) sugar
3 medium (US large) eggs, beaten
250ml/9fl oz soured cream
1 tsp vanilla extract

For the icing and decoration:
100g/3½oz plain (semi-sweet)
    chocolate, finely chopped
150g/5oz/1¼ sticks unsalted
    butter, softened
125g/4oz cream cheese
175g/6oz/heaping 1⅓ cups icing
    (confectioners') sugar, sifted
50g/2oz chocolate curls **45**,
    lightly crushed
Foil-covered chocolate eggs

Per slice: 590 cals; 42g fat (of which 25g saturates); 50g carbohydrate; 0.7g salt

1 Preheat the oven to 180°C (160°C fan oven)/350°F/Gas mark 4. Grease a 20.5cm/8in springform tin (pan) and line **1** with greaseproof (wax) paper, then grease the paper lightly. Sift the flour, cocoa powder, baking powder and salt into a large bowl.

2 Using an electric mixer or electric beaters, mix the butter and muscovado (brown) sugar **2** in a separate bowl until pale and fluffy – about 5 minutes. Gradually add the beaten eggs, mixing well after each addition. Add a little of the flour mixture if the butter mixture looks like curdling. In one go, add the remaining flour mixture, the soured cream and vanilla extract, then fold everything together gently with a metal spoon. Spoon into the prepared tin and bake for 40–50 minutes until a skewer inserted into the centre comes out clean **3**. Cool in the tin.

3 To make the icing, melt the chocolate **40** in a heatproof bowl set over a pan of barely simmering water, making sure the base of the bowl doesn't touch the water. Leave to cool for 15 minutes. In a separate bowl, beat the butter and cream cheese with a wooden spoon until combined. Beat in the icing (confectioners') sugar, then the cooled chocolate. Take care not to over-beat the mixture – it should be fudgey, not stiff.

4 Remove the cake from the tin, cut in half horizontally **4** and use some icing to sandwich the layers together. Transfer to a cake stand, then ice the top and sides, smoothing with a palette knife (metal spatula). Decorate with crushed chocolate curls **45** and chocolate eggs.

Coffee and Praline Celebration Gateau

Cuts into 8 slices

Preparation time: 45 minutes
Cooking time: 25 minutes, plus cooling

50g/2oz/½ stick unsalted butter, melted, plus extra to grease
125g/4oz/scant 1 cup plain (all-purpose) flour, sifted, plus extra to dust
4 large (US extra-large) eggs, separated
125g/4oz/½ cup caster sugar
1 tbsp coffee granules, dissolved in 2 tsp boiling water

For the praline:
50g/2oz/⅓ cup whole blanched hazelnuts
150g/5oz/⅔ cup caster sugar

For the filling:
500g/1lb 2oz mascarpone cheese
250g/9oz/2 cups icing (confectioners') sugar, sifted
2 tbsp coffee granules, dissolved in 1 tbsp boiling water

Per slice: 548 cals; 21g fat (of which 10g saturates); 83g carbohydrate; 0.2g salt

1 Preheat the oven to 190°C (170°C fan oven)/375°F/Gas mark 5. Grease two 18cm/7in loose-based sandwich tins (pans). Dust lightly with flour and tip out the excess.

2 Put the egg whites into a clean, grease-free bowl and whisk until soft peaks form. Whisk in 1 egg yolk; repeat with the other 3 yolks. Add the sugar, 1 tbsp at a time, and continue to whisk. The mixture should be thick enough to leave a trail when the whisk is lifted. Using a large metal spoon, fold half the flour into the mixture **2**.

3 Mix the coffee into the melted butter, then pour around the edge of the egg mixture. Add the remaining flour and gradually fold in. Divide the mixture between the prepared tins and bake for 25 minutes or until risen and firm to the touch **3**. Turn out on to a wire rack and leave to cool completely.

4 To make the praline **52**, line a baking sheet with non-stick baking parchment and scatter the nuts on it. Dissolve the sugar in a heavy-based pan over a low heat, shaking the pan once or twice to help it dissolve evenly. Cook until it forms a dark golden-brown caramel. Pour over the nuts and leave to cool.

5 To make the filling, put the mascarpone and icing (confectioners') sugar into a large bowl, add the coffee and mix with a hand-held electric whisk. Slice each cake in half horizontally **4**. Put one cake layer on a plate and spread with a quarter of the filling. Continue layering in this way, finishing with a layer of mascarpone filling.

6 Break the praline into two or three pieces and put into a plastic bag. Using a rolling pin, smash it into smaller pieces. Use to decorate the top of the cake.

Black Forest Roulade

Cuts into 10 slices

Preparation time: 35 minutes
Cooking time: 20 minutes, plus cooling and chilling

125g/4oz plain (semi-sweet)
    chocolate (at least 70% cocoa
    solids)
4 large (US extra-large) eggs,
    separated
125g/4oz/½ cup golden caster
    sugar, plus extra to dust
Cocoa powder and icing
    (confectioners') sugar to dust
Chocolate curls **45** to decorate
    (optional)

For the filling:
140ml/4½fl oz whipping cream
1 tsp icing (confectioners') sugar
75g/3oz Greek-style yogurt
2 × 425g/15oz cans morello
    cherries, drained, pitted
    and halved

PER SLICE: 248 cals; 12g fat (of which 7g saturates); 33g carbohydrate; 0.1g salt

1 Break the chocolate into pieces, melt **40** and leave to cool a little. Preheat the oven to 180°C (160°C fan oven)/350°F/Gas mark 4. Line **1** a 33 × 23cm/13 × 9in Swiss roll tin (jelly roll pan) with greaseproof (wax) paper or baking parchment.

2 Whisk the egg yolks with the sugar in a large bowl until thick and creamy. Whisk in the melted chocolate. Whisk the egg whites in a clean, grease-free bowl until stiff peaks form. Fold into the chocolate mixture **2**. Pour into the prepared tin, level the surface and bake for 20 minutes or until firm to the touch **3**. Leave to cool in the tin for 10–15 minutes.

3 Put a sheet of greaseproof paper or baking parchment on the work surface and dust with caster sugar. Carefully turn out the roulade on to the parchment and peel off the lining paper. Cover with a damp cloth and leave to cool for 30 minutes.

4 To make the filling, lightly whip the cream with the icing (confectioners') sugar, then fold in the yogurt. Spread over the cold roulade and scatter the cherries on top. Using the greaseproof paper or baking parchment to help, roll up the roulade from one of the narrow ends. Chill for 30 minutes. Dust with cocoa powder and icing sugar, decorate with chocolate curls **45**, if you like, and serve sliced.

White Chocolate and Orange Wedding Cake

Cuts into 30 slices

Preparation time: 1½ hours
Cooking time: 1 hour

Butter to grease
550g/1¼lb./3⅔ cups strawberries

For the large cake:
6 large (US extra-large) eggs,
    separated
250g/9oz/1 cup caster sugar
150g/5oz/1 cup self-raising
    (self-rising) flour
150g/5oz/1 cup ground almonds
Grated zest of 2 oranges

For the medium and small cakes:
4 large (US extra-large) eggs,
    separated
165g/5½oz/¾ cup caster sugar
125g/4oz/scant 1 cup self-raising
    (self-rising) flour
125g/4oz/1 cup ground almonds
Grated zest of 1¼ oranges

For the syrup:
200g/7oz/1 cup granulated sugar
500ml/18fl oz sweet white wine
Juice of 6 large oranges

For the white chocolate ganache:
400g/14oz white chocolate,
    chopped
600ml/21fl oz, 300ml/10½fl oz and
    150ml/5fl oz cartons double
    (heavy) cream

1   Preheat the oven to 180°C (160°C fan oven)/350°F/ Gas mark 4. Grease and base-line **1** a deep, round 23cm/9in cake tin (pan), a 15cm/6in cake tin and a 200g/7oz clean baked-bean tin (can) with greaseproof (wax) paper.

2   To make the large cake, put the egg whites into a clean, grease-free bowl and whisk until soft peaks form. Gradually beat in 50g/2oz/¼ cup sugar. Whisk until the mixture stands in stiff peaks and looks glossy.

3   Put the egg yolks and remaining sugar in another bowl and whisk until soft and moussey. Carefully stir in the flour to make a paste **2**.

4   Using a clean metal spoon, add a third of the egg white to the paste and fold in carefully. Put the remaining egg white, the ground almonds and orange zest into the bowl and fold in, taking care not to knock too much volume out of the egg white. You should end up with a smooth batter.

5   Spoon into the prepared 23cm/9in tin and bake for 35 minutes or until a skewer inserted into the centre comes out clean **3**.

6   Cool in the tin for 10 minutes, then turn out on to a wire rack and leave to cool completely. Make the other two cakes in the same way, gradually beating in 25g/1oz/⅛ cup of the sugar at step 2. Pour a quarter of the batter into the baked bean tin and the remaining mixture into the 15cm/6in cake tin. Bake the medium cake for 30–35 minutes and the small cake for 25–30 minutes. Turn out and cool as before.

7   Put the syrup ingredients into a pan and stir over a gentle heat until the sugar has dissolved. Bring to the boil and bubble for 5 minutes or until syrupy. Cool and set aside.

8   To make the ganache, put the chocolate into a heatproof bowl with half the cream. Set over a pan of simmering water, making sure that the base of the bowl doesn't touch the water, and leave until the chocolate has melted **40**, then stir. Don't stir the chocolate until it has completely melted. Leave to cool until beginning to thicken, then beat with a wooden spoon until cold and thick. Put the remaining double (heavy) cream into a bowl and whip lightly. Beat a large spoonful of the whipped cream into the chocolate cream to loosen it, then fold in the remainder. Cover and leave to chill for 2 hours.

9   Cut the cakes in half horizontally **4**, pierce all over with a skewer and put them, cut-sides up, on an edged tray or baking sheet. Spoon the syrup over and leave to soak in.

10   Hull and thinly slice the strawberries. Spread a quarter of the ganache over the base cakes and scatter with 425g/15oz/scant 8 cups strawberries. Cover with the top half of each cake and press down lightly. Using a palette knife, smooth the remaining ganache over the top and sides of the cakes. Assemble up to 4 hours ahead, wrap loosely and keep chilled in the fridge. Decorate with the remaining strawberries and serve.

Variation

Single-tiered celebration cake: Make the larger cake only, then split it and drizzle with syrup made with 100g/3½oz/½ cup golden granulated sugar, 250ml/ 8fl oz sweet white wine and the juice of 3 large oranges. Use 350g /12oz/2⅓ cups strawberries for the filling and decoration. Fill, then cover, with ganache made from 225g/8oz white chocolate and a 568ml/20fl oz carton double (heavy) cream.

PER SLICE: 530 cals; 34g fat (of which 17g saturates); 49g carbohydrate; 0.3g salt

Suppliers

UK

The Baker's Cupboard
www.thebakerscupboard.co.uk
01924 465 305

Cakes, Cookies & Crafts
www.cakescookiesandcraftsshop.co.uk
01524 389 684

Cake Craft
www.cakecraft.co.uk
02380 269 399

Cake Craft Shop
www.cakecraftshop.co.uk
01732 463 573

The Cake Decorating Company
www.thecakedecoratingcompany.
co.uk
0115 969 9800

Cake Decorating Store
www.cakedecoratingstore.co.uk
0845 652 5357

Cake Decorating Supplies
www.cakedecoratingsupplies.co.uk
0800 954 6948

Cake Maker Suppliers
www.cakemakersupplies.co.uk
0845 459 5095

Cake Stuff
www.cake-stuff.com
01555 890 111
Hobbycraft
www.hobbycraft.co.uk
0330 026 1400

Lakeland
www.lakeland.co.uk
015394 88100

The Little Cake Shop
www.thelittlecakeshop.co.uk
020 8871 0105

The Sugar Shack
www.sugarshack.co.uk
020 8204 2994

Canada

Cake Mischief
www.cakemischief.com
1-780-729-6990

Canadian Cake Decorators Guild
www.canadiancakedecorators.com

Golda's Kitchen
www.goldaskitchen.com
1-905-816-9995

J. Wilton
www.j-wilton.com
1-780-466-3174

McCall's
www.mccalls.ca
1-905-602-9622

US

Cakery Supplies
www.cakerysupplies.com
1-810-715-9823

Global Sugar Art
www.globalsugarart.com
1-800-420-6088
Kitchen Krafts
www.kitchenkrafts.com
1-800-298-5389

Ultimate Baker
www.cooksdream.com
1-425-369-9209

US Cake Supply
www.uscakesupply.com
1-858-909-2110

Australia

Baking Pleasures
bakingpleasures.com.au

Cake Deco
www.cakedeco.com.au
03 9654 5335

Cakes Around Town
www.cakesaroundtown.com.au
07 3160 8728

KWare
www.kware.com.au
1 300 552 202

Lollipop Cake Supplies
www.lollipopcakesupplies.com.au
07 3102 1246

First published in the United Kingdom in 2014 by Collins & Brown
10 Southcombe Street
London
W14 0RA

An imprint of Anova Books Company Ltd

Distributed in the US and Canada by Sterling Publishing Co, Inc.
387 Park Avenue South, New York, NY 10016-8810

A CIP catalogue for this book is available from the British Library

978-1-90939-717-0

10 9 8 7 6 5 4 3 2 1

Reproduction by Rival
Printed by 1010 Printing International Ltd, China

This book can be ordered direct from the publisher at www.anovabooks.com

Photography by: Martin Brigdale (pages 16, 23 and 122); Nicki Dowey (pages 25, 87, 101, 117
and 121); William Lingwood (pages 6 (T), 7, 9, 13, 17, 20 (B), 30, 36, 38, 39 (R), 40 (BL and BR),
41, 42, 43 (B), 44, 46, 47, 48, 54, 65, 68, 69, 71, 75, 76, 82, 83, 84, 85 (B), 86, 88, 90, 91, 92, 93,
94, 95, 98, 102, 104, 106, 108, 109, 110 and 111 (T)); Gareth Morgans (pages 51 and 53); Myles
New (page 119); Craig Robertson (pages 6 (B), 15, 18, 19, 20 (T), 21, 39 (L), 40 (TL and TR), 43
(TL and TR), 112, 113, 114 and 115); Lucinda Symons (pages 27, 28, 31, 60, 62, 63, 67, 72, 79,
85 (T), 89, 96 and 124); Martin Thompson (pages 22 and 58); Philip Webb (page 118).